M000316100

HEALTHY TREASURES COOKBOOK

HEALTHY TREASURES COOKBOOK

A BOUNTY OF FABULOUS TASTING RECIPES AND HEALTHY COOKING TIPS

ANNETTE REEDER

designed publishing

Designed Publishing
Glen Allen, VA 23059; 804.798.6565; www.designedhealthyliving.com

© 2012 by Annette Reeder. All rights reserved.

Artwork by Ellen Judy
Photo: Dennis Waterman
watermanphoto@yahoo.com
GlimpsesofHisCanvas.blogspot.com

No part of this publication may be reproduced, stored in a retrieval system, or transmitted in any way by any means—electronic, mechanical, photocopy, recording, or otherwise—without the prior permission of the copyright holder, except as provided by USA copyright law.

Scripture references marked NKJV are taken from the *New King James Version*. Copyright © 1982 by Thomas Nelson, Inc. Used by permission. All rights reserved.

Scripture references marked KJV are taken from the *King James Version* of the Bible.

Scripture references marked NIV are taken from the *Holy Bible, New International Version®, NIV®*. Copyright © 1973, 1978, 1984 by Biblica, Inc.™ Used by permission of Zondervan. All rights reserved worldwide. www.zondervan.com

Scripture references marked RSV are taken from the *Revised Standard Version* of the Bible, copyright 1952 [2nd edition, 1971] by the Division of Christian Education of the National Council of the Churches of Christ in the United States of America. Used by permission. All rights reserved.

ISBN 13: 13-9-7809853969-2-3
ISBN 10: 10-098539692-x
Library of Congress Catalog Card Number: 2010901623

Contents

"Unless we put medical freedom in the constitution, the time will come when medicine will organize into an undercover dictatorship...The constitution of this Republic should make special provision for medical freedom as well as religious freedom."

—Benjamin Rush M.D
signer of the Declaration of Independence 1745 -1813

I lovingly dedicate this book to my very precious and supportive family; my wonderful husband, Steve, my adventurous son Brent, his beautiful wife Mollie, their delightful daughters and our granddaughters, Lillie and Stella, and my cherished daughter Stacey along with her sincere husband Chris.

Welcome

Are you ready to fill your dinner table with rich tasting, health promoting foods? If you had recipes your family would love and enjoy, would that interest you? Then you have picked up the right book. In these pages are cooking tips, shopping guidelines, and over 250 recipes to help convert ordinary meals into ones with more satisfaction, satiety and sense of wellbeing than ever imagined.

What started me on the journey to this healthy treasure was our family's deteriorating health. We appeared normal but were sick inside our bodies. Our meals were the typical American diet—processed, processed, processed, and our health became processed also with numerous doctor visits, prescriptions, and side effects. Enough was enough; we were ready for change.

I was very blessed to have a good friend recommend reading *What the Bible Says about Healthy Living* by Dr. Rex Russell. This book led my family to remarkable health improvements and an enhanced lifestyle, which in turn encouraged me to further my education in nutrition and begin the Designed Healthy Living classes with the *Treasures of Healthy Living* Bible Study.

It is my joy that you have decided to grab your mixing bowl and shake your measuring spoons to discover this treasure. From this cookbook, you will gain many tasty recipes, along with numerous pages of healthful tips to make wise choices throughout your entire home.

Have fun. Enjoy the life God has given you. I wish you many blessings!

—Annette Reeder

Special Thanks

If a foodie is a person who loves food and all that goes with it, then this book has contributions both in recipes and in food tasting from a fabulous fun foodie group. From family heirloom favorites being transformed into a new healthy dish, to new innovative creations from kitchens all around the U.S., this cookbook is truly a bounty of many flavorful variations. Numerous people were in on the first Designed Healthy Living classes before the idea became published. These were the foundational friends and foodies who brought this book to life. *Treasures of Healthy Living Bible Study* and *Treasure of Health Nutrition Manual* soon followed. Without these friendships and foodies, this dream would not be in your hands today.

Special thanks goes to Nancy Nash and many others for their contributions from editing, tasting and overall insight. Everyone was very encouraging and eager to engage in an experiment with food based on biblical nutrition.

Food began in the Garden of Eden as a gift from our all-loving God and that is where the true acknowledgements begin. I know by the words He has given us that His gifts of health come from these foods. And I am never finished until I give thanks my Savior, Jesus Christ, who allowed me the joy of knowing Him and experiencing His love. It is because of Him that I have the blessing and the opportunity to prayerfully make a difference in other people's lives.

Taste and see that the Lord is good, blessed is the man who trusts in Him.
—Psalm 34:8

Blessings to your health,
Annette Reeder

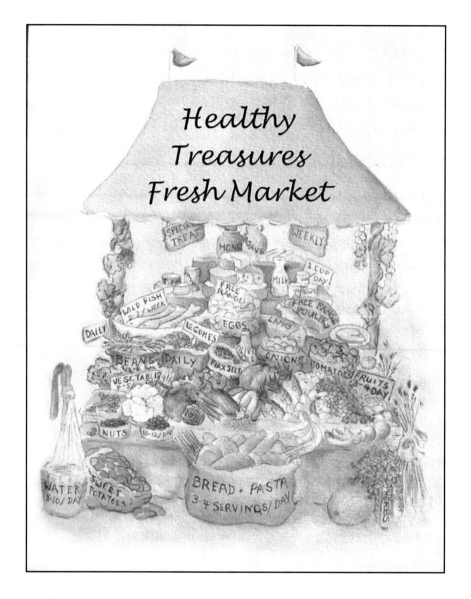

The Healthy Treasures Fresh Market is the foundation for our eating plan. Whole grains, fruits, vegetables, nuts, and beans are the very basis around which our daily diet needs to be built. Each day, our diet should include 3-4 servings of whole grains, 9 servings of fruits and vegetables, yogurt, water, and herbs with just a touch of meat protein. On special occasions, delight in a sweet treat and enjoy the goodness of honey, sugar cane, or agave nectar. This foundational pyramid will build a strong immune system, healthy bones, and a future of promise.

Setting Up Your Kitchen: The Right Tools

Before going to the grocery store or reading every recipe, look in the cabinets and investigate your supply of utensils and bakeware. Some cookware will contribute to health, while others will harm your health.

COOKWARE:

Aluminum—Use caution. Studies on aluminum are conflicting as to whether or not this contributes to mental problems. The safest option is to avoid this type of cookware.

> Food stored in the refrigerator is best in glass containers and not aluminum foil. Avoid using baking powder with aluminum.

Glassware—Pyrex glass loaf pans, pie plates, and cake pans are readily available in most stores. Glass is a heat insulator and not a heat conductor, which means glassware used on the stove top is not efficient. Glassware of newer varieties can also chip, shatter or break.

Teflon—The coating on this cookware can scratch or peel off into the food. This causes numerous health problems, and should be avoided.

Cephalon—A form of aluminum; caution should be taken with this product.

Stainless Steel—Generally a good cookware choice, but on its own is not a good heat conductor. High quality stainless steel cookware uses aluminum in the core, with stainless steel covering that core.

Waterless, greaseless stainless steel—This is the very best choice. Look for a high quality, lifetime waterless cookware for pots and pans. They are admittedly expensive, but you will gain the value in your health and a lifetime of use. I have had my set since 1980, and it looks great and cooks very well. The valve on several lids needed to be replaced a few years ago, and the company handled the replacement for free.

How the waterless, greaseless cookware works:

- The cookware is designed to cook fresh and frozen vegetables (and some fruits) with very little added water—just about 1 ounce of water per quart (30 ml/.95 L). This cooking method greatly reduces the loss of nutrients that occurs in other cooking methods, and the vegetables taste great!
- Nearly all of your meats, fish, and poultry cook without anyadded grease, fat, or cooking oil. This system can help you reduce calories without dieting, lower your cholesterol level, and maintain a healthy heart.
- Stack cooking lets you cook with more pans than you have burners. You'll especially appreciate this cookware when you are cooking for a large family gathering or a holiday dinner. The various combinations of cookware allow you to cook a number of foods on a single burner, saving energy and money.

Bakeware—Look for stainless steel bakeware.

Blender—All shapes and models of blenders are available in stores and online. My favorites are The Magic Bullet for personal drink sizes and the Bosch blender for larger servings. For sumptuous juice made from whole fresh vegetables and fruit, another favorite is the Vita Mix blender.

Utensils—Throw away the plastic utensils that melt when you use them. Get stainless steel for the same health benefits previously listed. Utensils made of wood are also a good choice.

Intriguing Ingredients

Ingredients in this cookbook may be new to you, so here are some explanations and common substitutions.

SWEETENERS

Sugar/sucanat—Sugar cane was created to grow naturally with nutrients and fiber. Processing and bleaching sugar removes these nutrients, thereby making it an expense to our health. A better choice would be sucanat. Sucanat is dried sugar cane with all the nutrition intact. Sucanat comes in names such as honey crystals, savannah gold, sucanat natural, and sucanat with honey.

Sucanat natural has a molasses flavor and is good for baking. The other varieties are lighter in color and have a mild flavor. The lighter type is good for drinks, cooking, and all ways in which we typically use white sugar. All varieties of sucanat can be substituted for regular white sugar in any recipe.

Sucanat with honey = Savannah Gold and Honey Crystals or white sugar
Sucanat natural = Sucanat or brown sugar

Healthy sugar replacements include: honey, molasses, date sugar, fruit concentrates, and agave.

Agave nectar is a healthy choice for a sweetener because it is sweeter than sugar, has fewer calories, contains inulin (a probiotic powder great for digestion), is low on the glycemic index, and is versatile and easy to cook.

It contains calcium, iron, and other vitamins and minerals. Agave nectar has run into some controversy with some "health experts," but not all agaves are alike. The highest quality brand is Xagave and can be found in some stores and restaurants. Agave is also available on line at www.xagave.com.

Dairy

Milk—Pasteurized, homogenized milk can be easily replaced with a higher quality milk such as almond, soy, rice, or raw milk. If you are going to purchase soy and dairy milk, always obtain the organic variety.

Rice Milk—Rice milk triggers less allergic reactions than soy milk.

Soy Milk—Soy milk provides a rich feel and taste to recipes, sauces, and baked puddings.

Raw Milk—Some people are sensitive to the pasteurization process and not the lactose. Many nutritionists recommend using raw milk, but be certain of its source. If the dairy is dirty, when you drink raw milk, you risk introducing bacteria into your body. Raw milk from a clean dairy carries with it a natural boost because of its calcium content.

Buttermilk—Buttermilk can be used in most recipes using milk. (You can make your own buttermilk using 1 cup of any type of milk and adding 1 tablespoon of lemon juice or apple cider vinegar. Let it sit for 5 minutes.)

Almond Milk—Nuts are often used to produce a "milk" product. Due to their lower fat content and digestibility, almonds are a favorite for being used in this way.

Powdered Milk—Powdered soy and rice milk are now available. Be sure to check the list of ingredients to avoid stabilizers and preservatives.

Juice—In some baked dishes, such as muffins, fruit juices can be used in place of milk. Even water can be used where fruit flavor is not wanted. Juice needs to be natural and from fruits grown in the USA, i.e. Florida Orange Juice.

Butter/Margarine—Now recognized as a product far worse than butter, margarine is a hydrogenated or partially hydrogenated fat. This means it contains trans-fats, which are detrimental to our health. There are new spreads out on the market claiming no trans fats, but still they are the result of a lab experiment. Don't risk it, go for the real organic butter.

Oil—Many times olive oil or canola oil can be used in place of butter. Be sure the oil is expeller pressed, first cold pressed, and/or extra virgin.

Better Butter—To cut the dairy in half, a better butter can be made. Use 1 part softened butter (not melted) and 1 part water. Whip by hand or in a food processor until creamy. This will remain soft like margarine. Oil can be used instead of water.

Yogurt—Yogurt can be made at home; but if purchasing a store brand, the label should state how many live cultures are included. Six to eight cultures in a yogurt product is a good amount. Popular brands are Stoneyfield, Brown Cow, and Nancy's.

Yo-cheese—Yo-cheese is strained yogurt using a coffee filter paper or a manufactured yogurt strainer. (I find the purchased yogurt strainer convenient to use.) Since yogurt is a healthy dairy choice for recipes, yo-cheese acts as an alternative for sour cream and cream cheese, and as stated above, you can make your own by straining yogurt.

To make yo-cheese, start by placing plain yogurt (vanilla yogurt can be used where a sweetened cream cheese is needed) in a cheesecloth lined strainer. Coffee filters will also work. Place the strainer over a bowl and refrigerate. Keeping the yogurt cold stops the fermenting process. Let the yogurt drain for 6 to 24 hours; the longer the time, the thicker the yo-cheese will be. Use yo-cheese as an alternative in any recipe calling for cream cheese, even cheesecakes. The yo-cheese will keep for one week. The whey that drains from the yogurt can be used in soups. Store in refrigerator. Straining one cup (240 ml) of yogurt will give you less than one cup of cheese. The longer you strain the less amount of cheese you will have, since the whey is draining from it. I recommend starting with 2 cups (470 ml) of yogurt.

Whipping cream—Raw certified whipping cream, or coconut milk

Sour Cream—Use nonfat sour cream or make your own, similar to cream cheese and yo-cheese. Sour cream must be strained for 2 hours and no more.

Cream Cheese—When purchasing from the store, choose lite or Neufchatel cheese.

Eggs—A combination of ground flaxseeds and water will provide a gelatinous substance that can work in place of eggs. To be sure you are purchasing eggs containing no antibiotics or hormones; obtain them from farms which raise range-fed hens.

FAT AND OILS:

Most people are aware of the fact that they need to cut back on fat. However, those same people are often uninformed of the hazards of some fat replacements. Trading one problem for another is not an example of effective problem solving. The alternatives we choose must be healthy choices if we're to experience long term benefits.

It is important to understand how oil is made. Most vegetable oils found in supermarkets are produced by using solvents, as in petroleum oil. The solvent is then burned off, producing a highly processed toxin (something that is poison to your body). Vegetable oils may be light in color, but most are poisonous to your body.

Expeller Pressed or Cold Pressed—These oils are made by pressing the oil from the seed, nut, or bean. No chemicals or solvents are used. These oils are left unrefined, or can be refined to produce additional stability for cooking. The expeller pressed oils have wonderful flavors and smaller amounts can produce excellent results. The best choice would be to find some of these expeller pressed oils in the organic form. Most of these oils need to be stored in the refrigerator to prevent rancidity, but olive oil can be stored in a dark cabinet away from light and heat.

Oil in Baking—Applesauce can replace oil in many recipes.

Oil in Marinades or Dressings—To replace all or part of the oil in salad dressings or marinades, use vegetable broth, chicken broth, or unsweetened fruit juice.

Oil for Sautéing—Sautéing can be done with broth, water, stock, or fruit juice.

GRAINS:

All grains have different flavors and may vary in texture. Some flour/grains are whole wheat pastry flour, whole wheat flour, brown rice flour, oat flour, spelt, kamut, etc.

Cereal—Cereal is a staple for breakfast in many homes. A few better choices than most store-bought cereal would include eating whole grain cereals with nuts, dried berries, no added sugars, and very little salt.

Flaxseed—Flaxseed is the richest source of Omega 3 fatty acids. It can be found in most stores, but the seeds have a much higher quality of omegas than the oil already made. It is best to grind seeds in a blender or coffee grinder each day. Flaxseed, once ground, is very beneficial to the diet of everyone in your family. A minimum amount to use is 2 tablespoons ground per person per day. Only purchase the seeds, and grind them yourself. The ground flaxseed in the stores has already lost its nutrition value. The quality of the flaxseed oil is critical to its effectiveness. If you choose to use the oil, make sure it is an organic and has not expired.

Nuts—Nuts have a high fat content, but this is a healthy monosaturated fat that is able to be utilized in the body. The quantity of nuts can be reduced without impacting a recipe. Toasting nuts prior to use makes the flavor stand out more, thereby lowering the quantity needed. Purchase unroasted, raw, unsalted nuts.

Beans—Beans come in all varieties and can easily be exchanged in a recipe. It is best not to substitute lentils for beans and vise versa.

Oats—Oats come in various qualities. Steel cut oats are the least processed and require the longest cooking time. Old-fashioned (rolled) oats is the typical long-cooking variety found in most stores. Quick oats require little cooking time, while instant oats are typically combined with sugar and artificial flavors and are the most processed. Keep in mind: the longer the cooking time required, the higher nutritional value. Recipes will state either old-fashioned or quick oats.

BAKING INGREDIENTS:

Baking Powder—Non-aluminum, low sodium, Rumford baking powder is a good brand, but there may be others.

Cornstarch—Arrowroot powder or an organic non-GMO cornstarch is now available in most stores.

Salt—Use unrefined mineral salt or sea salt. Good brands are RealSalt or a Celtic Salt.

Chocolate—High quality dark chocolate (60% or more cocoa) will enhance a recipe's health value, while milk chocolate is a far lesser quality, almost to the extent of a junk food. For chocolate chips, choose dark chocolate, carob, or grain sweetened.

Lecithin—Lecithin oil is valuable to the body. It aids the lubrication of joints, the absorption of vitamins A and D, the use of vitamins E and K, and assists in the transmission of messages from one nerve to another. It can also retard liver deterioration. Lecithin can be purchased as a powder, liquid, or granules. It is easy to add this to many dishes.

Coconut—Opt for unsweetened or dried coconut.

Jell-O®—Use unflavored gelatin. Employ fruit juices to make your own dessert.

Fruit Juices—Go for unsweetened, fresh pressed juices.

Canned fruits—Look for fruit canned in its own juice without the use of sweeteners or artificial sweeteners.

Frozen fruits—Opt for unsweetened frozen fruits.

Dried fruits—Eat unsulfured and unsweetened dried fruits.

Jams, jellies—It's pretty simple to find 100% all fruit spreads or honey sweetened spreads.

Meat—In most recipes beef, lamb, turkey, venison, and chicken can be interchanged to add variety to your menu or to match your supply. Recipes will state if a different meat is not appropriate. If a stock liquid is required in the recipe, then it will need to be changed to bring out the best flavor of the meat.

Stock liquid—The best matched stock liquid will bring out the richest flavor in the recipe. Generally chicken dishes taste best when combined with a vegetable or chicken stock. For a beef dish, use a beef stock as your first choice. Turkey can be accompanied by chicken, turkey, or vegetable stock.

GENERAL TIPS FOR HEALTHY COOKING

A good quality set of waterless, stainless steel cookware can reduce the oil necessary to sauté and cook. It will also reduce the cooking time. Do not use coated cookware, since the coating can leach or peel off into your food and be very toxic to your body. More about this is discussed under "Setting up Your Kitchen with the Right Tools" and the Resource Section.

Replace ¼ to ½ of ground meats with cooked grains (brown rice, bulgur, barley) to reduce the cholesterol and fat. This also adds fiber to the recipe.

Pureed, cooked vegetables such as carrots, squash, pumpkin, or potatoes, can thicken soups and sauces. These purees can be used in place of cream, egg yolks, and flour.

BEGINNINGS OF GOOD HEALTH
PURE WATER

The 10 Commandments of Good Hydration

1. Drink ½ ounce (15 ml) of water daily for every pound (454 grams) you weigh.
2. Avoid diuretic beverages that flush water out of your body such as caffeinated coffee, tea, soda, alcohol, and beer.
3. Drink more water and fresh juices to maintain hydration during illness and upon recovery. Illness robs your body of water.
4. Start your day with ½ to 1 quart (470-940 ml) of water to flush your digestive tract and rehydrate your system from the overnight fast.
5. Drink water at regular intervals throughout the day. Don't wait until you're thirsty.
6. Get in the habit of carrying a water bottle with you. Keep one in the car or on your desk. Convenience helps. Use a water purifier in your home and refill a quality bottle to take with you.

7. Make a habit of drinking water. Decide to drink water at least 30 minutes before every meal. Take water breaks instead of coffee breaks.
8. Increase your drinking when you increase your mental activity level, your stress level, and your exercise level.
9. Drink the purest water available.
10. Perspire. Exercise to the point of perspiration or enjoy a steam bath. Sweat cleans the lymphatic system and bloodstream. It is one of the best detoxification avenues available to us. Do drink plenty of water afterwards to replace the loss of fluids. Drink more water in hot weather.

Wise choice: Use a Reverse Osmosis system in your home that has a three stage technology to get rid of the most contaminants.

Appealing

Appetizers

Baked Asparagus Dip

- » 1 pound (454 grams) diced cooked fresh asparagus—drained
- » 1 cup (240 ml) grated parmesan cheese
- » 1 cup (240 ml) safflower mayonnaise

1. Preheat oven: 375°F (190°C).

2. In large bowl, combine the asparagus, cheese, and mayonnaise.

3. Place in a 2 cup (470 ml) oven-proof bowl.

4. Bake for 20 minutes or until heated through.

Serve with bread, crackers, or chips.

 *Buying Asparagus*

Look for bright green spears that are firm and straight with a uniform diameter (so that they will cook in the same amount of time). The tips should be compact and have a slightly purplish color.

Summertime Fruit Dip

- » 2 cups (470 ml) fresh peaches—sliced
- » 2 cups (470 ml) strawberries—sliced
- » 1 tablespoon lemon juice
- » ½ teaspoon almond extract
- » Assorted fresh fruit for dipping

1. In a food processor, combine fruit, lemon juice and extract; cover and process until smooth.

Serve with fruit.

Frozen fruit can be used—thaw before blending.

Bean Hummus

» 2-15 ounce (450 ml) cans red, pinto, chick peas or black beans—rinsed and drained
» ½ cup (120 ml) tahini
» ¼ cup (60 ml) lemon juice
» ¼ cup (60 ml) cilantro—chopped fresh
» ½ teaspoon cayenne pepper
» 4 green onions—sliced
» 2 tablespoons olive oil
» 2 large garlic cloves—minced
» 1 teaspoon cumin
» Salt and pepper to taste

1. Combine all ingredients in food processor until smooth.

2. Season to taste with salt and pepper.

Serve with chips, pita wedges, or baguettes.

 Tahini

Tahini is a fine paste made from grinding sesame seeds with all the nutrients intact. It is rich in vitamins, minerals, protein and essential fatty acids. Tahini can be added to sauces and salad dressings. You can also substitute it for butter on toast.

Flavorful Variations

* Hummus can be used as a sandwich spread, in pita pockets, on veggie wraps, and on salads. There are even more uses if you use your imagination. Replace mayonnaise in recipes with hummus. Adds protein and fiber.

Mexican Bean Dip

- » 2 cups (470 ml) pinto beans— mashed
- » 8 ounces (224 g) yo-cheese
- » 2 cups (470 ml) cheddar cheese—shredded
- » 1 cup (240 ml) Monterey jack cheese—shredded
- » 8 ounce (224 g) Salsa

1. Preheat oven: 350°F (180°C).

2. Layer bottom of dish with mashed pinto beans. Spread 8 ounce (224 g) yo-cheese (drained nonfat plain yogurt), on top of beans.

3. Cover with cheddar and Monterey jack cheese. Top with salsa.

4. Bake until cheese is melted. Serve with healthy chips.

Makes 4 servings.

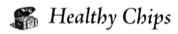 *Healthy Chips*

Choose chips that are organic and have no trans fats. Even though the package may say no trans fats, make sure ingredients do not include hydrogenated and partially hydrogenated oils.

Mexican Black Bean Dip (Salsa)

- » 2 cups (470 ml) black beans—cooked and cooled
- » 1 cup (240 ml) organic corn—frozen
- » 2 green onions—chopped
- » ½ cup (120 ml) purple onion—chopped
- » ¼ cup (60 ml) fresh Cilantro—washed and finely chopped
- » ¾ cup (180 ml) Grape tomatoes—halved
- » 7 tablespoons olive oil
- » 3 tablespoons cumin—ground
- » 3 limes—juiced

1. *Drain beans and corn and wash in colander. Place in bowl with remaining ingredients. Stir together and chill several hours before serving.*

Serve with chips or on a salad.

Makes 4 servings.

Flavorful Variations

* Substitute black-eyed peas and Italian dressing in place of black beans and olive oil
* Red peppers
* Omit cumin
* Replace limes with lemons

Fiesta Party Wraps

- » 1-8 ounce (224 g) package cream cheese—softened
- » 1-8 ounce (224 g) sour cream or yo-cheese
- » 1 garlic clove—minced
- » 1-4 ounce (112 g) can diced green chilies
- » 3 tablespoons green onions—chopped
- » ¼ cup (60 ml) Salsa
- » 16 ounce (448 g) grated cheddar cheese
- » 10 tortillas—whole wheat or sun dried tomato

1. *In a medium-size mixing bowl, combine cream cheese, sour cream, garlic, chilies, green onions, and salsa. Add cheese and mix well.*

2. *Spread the mixture onto tortillas. Roll the tortillas up and refrigerate for at least 1 hour.*

3. *Slice the tortilla rolls and serve.*

 ## Making your own Yo-Cheese

Use a good quality yogurt to make your own yo-cheese. Strain yogurt through a yogurt funnel. (You can also use a coffee filter or a yogurt funnel that can be purchased at specialty stores.) Strain for 20 minutes to make the equivalent to sour cream, or for several hours to make a cream cheese. This will give you better nutrition and a quality taste.

Basil Pesto

- » 2 cups (470 ml) fresh basil leaves
- » ½ cup (120 ml) parmesan cheese
- » ½ cup (120 ml) nuts (be creative and try pine nuts or soy beans)
- » ½ cup (120 ml) olive oil
- » 3 large garlic cloves
- » ⅛ teaspoon salt

1. *In food processor combine all ingredients. Store in refrigerator for up to 5 days.*

2. *Can be used to spread on bread, meat (marinade) or as a dip for chips and vegetables.*

Flavorful Variations

* ¼ cup (60 ml) sun dried tomatoes in oil and 2 tablespoons feta cheese
* Add poblano chili peppers, cilantro, and lime juice for a chipotle flavor.
* Cilantro can be used in place of basil. Cilantro helps the body remove heavy metals from its cells.

Storing homemade pesto

Store homemade pesto or hummus in an ice cube tray and refrigerate or freeze for later use. Then throw a frozen pesto cube in with your pasta, defrost it to spread on a sandwich or add a few to a roast. You will always have pesto on hand by storing extra in the freezer.

Refried Beans

» ¼ cup (60 ml) butter
» ¼ cup (60 ml) olive oil
» ¾ cup (180 ml) chopped onions
» 2 garlic cloves—minced
» 4 cups (960 ml) pinto beans—cooked
» 3 tablespoons chili powder
» 4 teaspoons ground cumin
» 2 teaspoons salt
» Pinch cayenne

1. *Sauté onions and garlic in butter and oil. Add cooked beans to onions and garlic.*

2. *Blend with mixer or blender. Add chili powder, cumin, salt and cayenne. Add water if needed for consistency.*

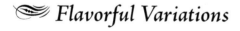 *Flavorful Variations*

* Black beans are a great substitute.

 *Cayenne*

Cayenne pepper has a pungent and fiery flavor. It has been noted to help heal arthritis, psoriasis and works as an anticoaglulant.

Stuffed Mushrooms

- » 12 mushrooms to fill—keep stems
- » 3 green onions—chopped
- » 2 cloves garlic—crushed
- » 1 teaspoon butter or olive oil
- » 4 slices turkey bacon—cooked in small pieces
- » ½ cup (120 ml) parmesan cheese
- » 12 ounce (336 g) lite cream cheese or Neufchatel
- » 1 teaspoon Natural Herb and Spice Seasoning

1. *Preheat oven: 350°F (180°C).*

2. *Pull out mushroom stems and chop small with green onions. Brown stems, onions, and garlic in 1 teaspoon butter or olive oil. Mix the remaining ingredients with the sautéed vegetables. Fill mushroom caps.*

3. *Place mushrooms, filled side up, in lightly oiled baking dish and bake approximately 12 minutes. Makes 6 servings.*

Toasted Grain

- » 1 pound (454 grams) whole wheat kernels
- » 1 teaspoon salt
- » Water
- » 1 teaspoon olive oil

1. *Heat a frying pan and pour in the kernels and salt. Stir constantly until lightly browned. Sprinkle a little water over while toasting to soften the seeds.*

2. *A little more olive oil may be necessary for flavor.*

Eat as you would popcorn.

Veggie Snack Bars

- » 1 bread dough for loaf*
- » 1 cup (240 ml) nonfat plain yo-cheese*
- » 8 ounces (224 g) lite cream cheese
- » 1 tablespoon Ranch Dressing Mix*
- » ½ cup (120 ml) grape tomatoes—quartered
- » ½ cup (120 ml) bell pepper— red, yellow, or green— chopped
- » 1 cup (240 ml) broccoli— chopped
- » ½ cup (120 ml) onion— chopped
- » 2 cups (470 ml) sharp cheddar cheese—shredded

*recipe included in this book.

1. *Preheat oven: 350°F (180°C).*

2. *Roll out about ⅓ of the prepared dough on sprayed 9" x 13" pan (like a cookie sheet). Let rise 30 minutes. Bake 8-10 minutes. Let cool.*

3. *Mix yo-cheese, cream cheese, and dressing mix. Spread on top of bread. Sprinkle the following on top of cheese mixture: Chopped grape tomatoes, bell pepper, broccoli, onion, and cheese. Refrigerate and serve as an appetizer or finger food.*

Makes 6 servings.

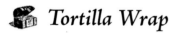 *Tortilla Wrap*

This can be spread on a tortilla and topped with vegetables or turkey, then rolled up. Refrigerate and slice into 1 inch pieces.

Note: The original recipe called for all cream cheese, but by using the yo-cheese the recipe will have less fat and more calcium and protein. The original recipe also calls for ranch dressing mix; however, making your own will avoid the MSG.

Spicy Warm Black Bean Dip

- » 1 small onion—chopped
- » 2 garlic cloves—minced
- » 1 teaspoon olive oil
- » 2 cups (470 ml) or one can black beans—rinsed
- » ½ cup (120 ml) tomato—diced
- » ⅓ cup (75 ml) salsa
- » ½ teaspoon ground cumin
- » ½ teaspoon chili powder
- » ¼ cup (60 ml) cheese, your choice, cheddar or farmers works well
- » ¼ cup (60 ml) minced fresh cilantro
- » 1 tablespoon lime juice
- » Chips

1. *In a large skillet, sauté onion and garlic in oil on medium low until tender. Add the beans; gently mash with fork. Stir in the tomato, salsa, cumin and chili powder.*

2. *Cook and stir just until heated through. Remove from heat; stir in cheese, cilantro, and lime juice. Serve warm with chips.*

 Garlic

Garlic is an excellent ingredient to add to your favorite dishes. The medical field has over 700 published studies on the health benefits found in garlic. Adding this herb to your foods may help with infections, sore throats, cancer, heart disease, bacteria, and sinus problems. Use fresh garlic to get the natural healing properties, versus the powder or store bought minced which only adds flavor.

Breakfast Bonanza

Breakfast Bonanza

Did you know bonanza means "a source that yields great riches or success"? A healthy breakfast and great start to the day will definitely yield success. In fact, it has been proven that kids who eat breakfast have better mental function, higher metabolism, more energy and perform better in school. These results are proof breakfast can be a bonanza.

Our digestive system needs success too. After a long 8-hour fast, a healthy breakfast rich with fiber will get our digestive system moving for the day. While we sleep, our bodies do a routine clean up and leave the trash ready for fiber to come along and sweep it out of the body. No fiber in the breakfast meal—no sweeping out of the trash. So, the trash will have to either go back to where it started or wait for fiber at lunch to move it along. Protein combined with fiber will provide satiety and maintain a healthy glucose level—a true bonanza.

High sugar breakfast contributes to kids and adults getting hungry early in the mid-morning and reaching for another sweet treat to hold them over till lunch. The best breakfast bonanza choice is a meal high in fiber and protein. There are several great selections in this section.

Better Butters

Honey Butter

Easy to make yourself.

- » ½ cup honey
- » ¼ cup butter softened

1. Place ingredients in the blender and blend until smooth. Store in refrigerator. Yummy!

Strawberry Butter

- » ½ cup (120 ml) fresh or drained thawed strawberries
- » ½ stick of butter
- » ⅓ cup (75 ml) honey

1. Blend in blender.

Flavorful Variations

* substitute cranberries, raspberries or blueberries in place of strawberries

Nut Butter

- » 2 cups (470 ml) cashews, almonds or peanuts—raw and unsalted
- » 3 tablespoons unrefined organic vegetable oil or oil of your choice, divided
- » ¼ teaspoon salt
- » 1 teaspoon honey, optional

1. Process nuts, 2 tablespoons oil, salt, and sugar or honey 30 seconds in high performance blender. Purée to spreading consistency, adding remaining oil if needed. Store in airtight container in the refrigerator. Makes 2 cups (470 ml).

Satisfying Syrups

Maple Syrup

- » 1½ cups (360 ml) water
- » 1 cup (240 ml) sucanat with honey or honey crystals
- » ½ cup (120 ml) honey
- » 1 tablespoon maple flavoring or vanilla

1. Combine water, sucanat, and honey in saucepan.

2. Bring to boil. Remove from heat and add flavoring.

Flavorful Variations

* blueberry, raspberry, strawberry, rhubarb

Chocolate Syrup

- » 1 cup (240 ml) agave or honey
- » 1 cup (240 ml) dark cocoa powder—organic
- » Dash salt
- » 1 cup (240 ml) water
- » 1 tablespoon vanilla

1. Mix agave or honey, cocoa, and salt in saucepan. Add water.

2. Bring to boil. Reduce heat and add vanilla. Cool and store in refrigerator.

Flavorful Variations

* For a hot or cold drink mix 2 tablespoons of syrup and 1 cup (240 ml) milk and then heat slowly for a warm drink. Or use as a syrup over ice cream. Shake well with each use.

Tasty Toppings

Fresh Fruit Topping

Great on pancakes, waffles, shortcake, and ice cream.

- » 2 cups (470 ml) fresh berries of your choice
- » ½ teaspoon vanilla
- » ¼ teaspoon cinnamon— optional

1. Blend 1 cup (240 ml) of berries in blender until smooth. In bowl combine pureed fruit, vanilla, cinnamon, and 1 cup (240 ml) chopped berries.

2. Mix well. Serve chilled or at room temperature.

Strawberry Topping

Serve over pancakes, waffles, yogurt, or ice cream

- » ½ cup (120 ml) fresh or frozen strawberries—crushed
- » ½ cup (120 ml) cold water
- » 2 tablespoons organic cornstarch
- » 2 tablespoons honey
- » 1½ cups (360 ml) fresh or frozen strawberries— quartered

1. Blend together the crushed strawberries, water, cornstarch and honey. Cook over medium heat, stirring constantly, until thickened and clear. Stir in the quartered strawberries and heat through.

Strawberries

Red, juicy and cone-shaped, the strawberry is a common berry to be grown by even the beginner gardener. Buy strawberries with the cap still on and do not remove or wash until ready to eat. Or better yet, eat the cap; it is loaded with phytonutrients.

Baked French Toast

- » 1 stick butter
- » 1 cup (240 ml) sucanat with honey or honey crystals
- » 6 slices whole wheat bread
- » 6 eggs
- » 1¼ cups (300 ml) milk
- » 1 teaspoon vanilla
- » 1 teaspoon salt
- » 1 tablespoon cinnamon

1. *Melt butter in 13" x 9" pan. Add sucanat to butter and spread over pan. Place bread slices in pan.*

2. *In mixing bowl, beat eggs. Add milk, vanilla, salt, and cinnamon. Pour egg mixture over bread slices. Refrigerate overnight.*

3. *In the morning Preheat oven: 350°F (180°C) Bake uncovered for 35-40 minutes. Top with fresh fruit, nuts, or maple syrup.*

Makes 8 servings.

Breakfast Casserole

- » 9 eggs—beaten
- » 2½ cups (590 ml) low-fat non-homogenized milk or soy milk
- » 1½ teaspoons dry mustard
- » 1 teaspoon salt
- » 3 slices whole wheat bread—cubed
- » 1½ cups (360 ml) cheddar cheese
- » 1 pound (454 grams) cooked and crumbled turkey sausage

1. *Mix all ingredients together and pour into 9" x 13" dish. Cover and refrigerator overnight.*

2. *Preheat oven: 350°F (180°C).*

3. *Bake uncovered for 1 hour. Cut in squares and serve hot.*

Makes 8 servings.

Breakfast Parfait

- » 1 cup (240 ml) quick oats
- » 2 cups (470 ml) vanilla yogurt
- » 1 8 ounce (224 g) can crushed pineapple, do not drain
- » 2 cups (470 ml) sliced strawberries, bananas, blueberries, or peaches
- » 2 tablespoons sliced almonds

1. *Combine oats, yogurt, and pineapple. Refrigerate overnight.*

2. *Layer oatmeal mixture with fruit and top with almonds. This will keep refrigerated for one week.*

Makes 8 servings.

Breakfast Pizza

- » 1 recipe Whole Wheat Honey bread dough*
- » 12 ounces (336 g) turkey sausage, cooked and crumbled
- » 1 cup (240 ml) braised potatoes
- » 1 cup (240 ml) cheese—grated
- » ¼ cup (60 ml) milk
- » 4 eggs
- » 2 tablespoons parmesan cheese

*recipe included in this book

1. *Preheat oven: 375°F (190°C).*

2. *Roll dough out in a deep, lightly greased, pizza pan. Top dough with sausage, potatoes, and cheese. Whisk milk and eggs together. Carefully pour milk mixture over sausage mixture. Sprinkle with parmesan cheese.*

3. *Bake for 25 minutes or until crust is brown.*

4. *Bread recipe will make two crusts so you may want to use the other half for a cinnamon roll.*

Makes 6 servings.

 Braised

Braised refers to cooking a meat or vegetable in a small amount of liquid—stock or olive oil in a covered pot. Potatoes can be braised by cutting in large chunks or slices, then basted in olive oil and garlic before placing in oven until browned.

Use roasted sweet potatoes or braised potatoes from recipes in this book.

Cream of Wheat

- » 2 cup (470 ml) water
- » ¼ cup (60 ml) milk
- » 3 tablespoons honey
- » ½ teaspoon blackstrap molasses
- » ¼ cup (60 ml) raisins
- » ¼ cup (60 ml) unsweetened coconut
- » 1 teaspoon cinnamon
- » 1 cup (240 ml) bulgur wheat
- » 1 teaspoon vanilla

1. *Bring water to boil. Add ingredients one at a time, adding bulgur last.*

2. *Cover and simmer for 20 minutes. Serve immediately.*

Makes 4—one cup servings.

Flavorful Variations

* Dried blueberries are a luscious option in place of, or in addition to, raisins.

Millet Cereal

- » 3 cups (720 ml) water
- » 1 cup (240 ml) millet
- » 2 tablespoons maple syrup
- » 1 apple—finely chopped
- » 1 teaspoon canola oil
- » 2 teaspoon vanilla
- » 1 teaspoon cinnamon

1. *Bring water to boil. Add millet and reduce heat.*

2. *Add remaining ingredients and simmer for 40 minutes.*

Makes 2-4 servings.

 ## Millet

Most often found in bird feeders, millet, which is rich in protein, has a bland flavor lending itself to a variety of seasonings. It can be prepared like rice by boiling water and used to make hot cereal. Ground millet can be used in bread, puddings and cakes.

Favorite Pancakes

- » 1 cup (240 ml) kamut flour
- » 1 teaspoon baking powder
- » ½ teaspoon salt
- » 2 tablespoons sucanat with honey
- » 1 egg
- » 1 cup (240 ml) milk
- » 2 tablespoons oil
- » Blueberries, pecans, walnuts, etc., optional

1. *Mix dry ingredients in one bowl; mix liquid ingredients in another and then combine. Pour onto lightly oiled griddle or waffle iron.*

2. *Enjoy with favorite topping or plain as is.*

Makes 6 servings.

 *Kamut*

Kamut, a close relative to wheat, is about the same shape as a wheat seed but more than twice as big. Many people who are wheat intolerant can eat Kamut with no problems. Kamut is a high nutrition food but is slightly lower in protein and gluten than regular wheat. Kamut can be used in place of all the different wheats—both the hard and soft varieties—and also durum wheat. Kamut has a distinct light yellow color when milled and can easily be disguised as a store-bought pancake mix!

Power Packed Pancakes

- » 1 egg
- » 1 cup (240 ml) milk
- » 1 tablespoon canola oil
- » 3 tablespoons wheat germ
- » ¾ cup (180 ml) flour—whole wheat, soft white—pastry, kamut, or spelt
- » ½ teaspoon salt
- » 1 teaspoon baking powder
- » 3 tablespoons protein powder
- » 1 ripe banana, other fruits can be added for variation

1. *Mix egg, milk, and oil; set aside. In separate bowl mix wheat germ, flour, salt and powders. Combine wet and dry ingredients lightly. There will be some small lumps. Mash the banana and add to mix.*

2. *Let sit 10 to 30 minutes to let flour become hydrated.*

Makes 10 to 12 pancakes, 6 inches in size.

 ## Olive, Safflower, and Canola Oil

When buying oils—look for "first cold pressed" or "expeller pressed" to ensure the highest quality. Oils should be in dark glass bottles or cans for better stability. Most oils should be refrigerated after opening to prevent rancidity. Olive oil is the most nutritious. Do not use any oils that smell rancid. All oils are best organic, especially Canola since it is commonly grown from a GMO seed. Olive oil is the best for stir frying and cooking on medium to low heat. If the oil begins to smoke while cooking, discard it and start over with fresh oil. Your health is worth it.

Fruitful Rice Pudding

- » 2 cups (470 ml) brown rice—cooked
- » 1 cup (240 ml) unsweetened, crushed pineapple
- » ¼ cup (60 ml) raisins
- » ¾ cup (180 ml) hot water
- » 1 ripe banana
- » 3 tablespoons orange juice
- » 1 teaspoon vanilla
- » ½ teaspoon almond extract
- » 2 tablespoons honey

1. Preheat oven: 350°F (180°C).

2. Mix rice, pineapple and raisins in an 8" x 8" casserole dish. Process remaining ingredients in a blender until smooth and pour over rice and fruit.

3. Bake for 45 minutes and serve hot.

4. This may be made ahead by baking for 30 minutes and reheating just before serving.

Garnish with peach or banana slices.

Overnight Oatmeal

"My youngest asked for more!" Simple to double for more servings.

- » 2 cups (470 ml) old-fashioned oats
- » 4½ cups (1.1 L) water
- » 1 teaspoon salt
- » 1 tablespoon butter
- » 1 teaspoon cinnamon*
- » 1 apple, cut into slivers*
- » Dash nutmeg*
- » Honey to taste*

* Optional ingredients

1. Spray crock pot with oil. Combine oats, water, salt and butter in crock pot.

2. Cook on low for 8 hours. Enjoy.

⤳ Flavorful Variations

* Add ½ cup (120 ml) nuts, ½ teaspoon cinnamon, ½-1 cup (120-240 ml) of any of these fruits; chopped apples, raisins, dates, and currants.

Muesli-Nut Fruit Salad

An easy alternative to breakfast cereals and a great dieter's breakfast

- » ½ cantaloupe
- » 1 apple
- » 1 mango
- » 1 banana
- » 2 peaches
- » 5 strawberries
- » ¼ cup (60 ml) old-fashioned oats
- » ¼ cup (60 ml) unsalted cashews, almonds, pecans, or walnuts
- » 4 tablespoons unsweetened, shredded coconut
- » 1 tablespoon sesame seeds
- » ⅛ teaspoon cinnamon
- » ½ cup (120 ml) raisins, dried blueberries, or dates
- » 2 cups (470 ml) non-fat yogurt

1. *Cut up fruit into bite size pieces; set aside. In a food processor, combine the oats, nuts, coconut, sesame seeds, and cinnamon.*

2. *Process with on/off turns until coarsely ground; do not over process or the mixture will become a paste.*

3. *Sprinkle over fruit. Stir in the dried fruit and top with yogurt.*

Makes 1-2 servings.

Flavorful Variations

* **Cold Cereal:** Soak ¼ cup (75 ml) muesli in ½ cup (120 ml) yogurt or fruit juice overnight. Enjoy as a quick, satisfying breakfast.
* **Hot Cereal:** Add ½ cup (120 ml) muesli to ½ cup (120 ml) water or milk and bring to boil. Simmer 3-5 minutes.

Muesli Mix

This recipe makes enough dry mix to keep on hand for a quick pick-me-up snack when added to yogurt or Kefir.

» 2 cups (470 ml) oats
» 1 cup (240 ml) mixed nuts—chopped
» ⅔ cup (150 ml) coconut
» ⅓ cup (75 ml) sesame seeds
» ⅓ cup (75 ml) flax seed
» 2 tablespoons cinnamon
» 1 cup (240 ml) dried blueberries—optional
» 1 cup (240 ml) dates or raisins

1. Mix and store in air tight container.

Swiss Muesli

» ½ cup (120 ml) water
» ½ cup (120 ml) old-fashioned oats
» 1 cup (240 ml) nonfat, unsweetened yogurt
» ½ cup (120 ml) raisins
» ¼ cup (60 ml) dried apricots—chopped
» 2 tablespoons natural bran
» 2 tablespoons oat bran
» 2 tablespoons flaxseed—ground
» 1 organic apple—cored and chopped
» 1 teaspoon cinnamon

1. Bring water to a boil. In a medium bowl, pour boiling water over old-fashioned oats. Let stand until water is absorbed, about 25 minutes. Add remaining ingredients. Mix well.

2. Cover and refrigerate.

Serve chilled. Keeps for 4 days.

Quiche

- » 1-9" whole wheat deep dish pie crust *
- » 1 tablespoon Dijon mustard
- » 1½ cups (360 ml) broccoli— steamed and diced
- » 2 cups (470 ml) cheese (your choice)—shredded
- » 1 cup (240 ml) milk
- » 4 eggs
- » ¼ teaspoon salt
- » ⅛ teaspoon cayenne pepper
- » ¼ teaspoon black pepper

*recipe in this book

1. *Bake shell at 425°F (220°C) for 8 minutes.*

2. *Spread mustard in pie shell. Sprinkle in broccoli and cheese over mustard. Whisk together eggs, milk, and seasonings. Pour over cheese and broccoli.*

3. *Bake at 375°F (190°C) for 45 minutes until a knife inserted in the center comes out clean.*

Let stand 10 minutes before slicing.

Flavorful Variations

* Turkey sausage (¾ cup (180 ml) cooked and crumbled) or one cup (240 ml) chicken along with ¼ cup (60 ml) chopped onion can be added.
* Spinach makes a tasty substitute for broccoli. Use frozen spinach, thawed and patted dry.

Choosing the Incredible, Edible Egg

Eggs are highly nutritious. Find a farmer who raises fresh eggs from hens that are able to scratch around in a yard and eat without the addition of antibiotics or hormones to their food. The taste of fresh eggs and the health benefits, including lecithin which helps normalize cholesterol, will amaze you. Enjoy the yolk and the whites together for a protein-packed nutritious benefit.

Spanish Eggs

» 2 tablespoons canola oil
» 2 green onions—chopped
» 1 fresh ripe tomato—chopped
» 6 eggs
» ¼ cup (60 ml) salsa or picante sauce
» Ground pepper and salt to taste
» 1 tablespoon fresh parsley or cilantro

1. In a skillet sauté onions and tomato in heated oil over medium heat until onions are soft (3 minutes). Reduce heat to low.

2. In a bowl combine eggs, salsa, pepper, and salt. Beat until frothy. Add to skillet.

3. Cook over low heat, stirring occasionally until almost set.

4. Add cilantro or parsley and stir until set.

Makes 3 servings.

Quick and Easy Granola

- » 1 stick butter
- » ½ cup (120 ml) honey
- » 1 teaspoon vanilla
- » 4 cups (960 ml) oats
- » Nuts, raisins, coconut

1. Preheat oven 400°F (200°C).

2. Melt together butter and honey. Add vanilla.

3. In separate bowl combine oats with your choice of nuts, raisins and coconut. Combine with melted butter and stir well to coat.

4. Place on cookie sheet or 9" x 13" pan. Bake for 20 minutes.

5. Stir and bake 10 or more minutes until crispness desired.

This can be used as cold cereal.

Makes 8 servings.

∽ Flavorful Variations

* To increase the nutrition and flavor, add any of the following ingredients in increments of ½ cup until you like the results; almonds, sunflower seeds, flax seeds, dried coconut, dried apples, cranberries, walnuts, cinnamon, chocolate chips, and protein powder.

Granola

- » 7 cups (1.7 L) quick oatmeal
- » 1 cup (240 ml) wheat germ
- » 1 cup (240 ml) coconut
- » 1 cup (240 ml) nuts
- » 1 teaspoon salt
- » 1 cup (240 ml) sucanat with honey or natural
- » ½ cup (120 ml) olive oil
- » ½ cup (120 ml) water
- » 1 tablespoon vanilla

1. *Preheat oven: 275°F (140°C).*

2. *Stir together first 5 ingredients in a large bowl. In smaller bowl, mix last ingredients. Pour liquid mixture into oat mixture. Mix thoroughly until oats are moist.*

3. *Bake in shallow pan for 1 hour. Stir after 30 minutes.*

Flavorful Variations

* Various dried fruit can be added for selection and savor. For softer granola, shorten baking time. For more crunch, increase baking time.

Chewy Breakfast Bars

A perfect breakfast on the go or a snack on hand.

- » 3 cups (720 ml) old-fashioned oats
- » 1 cup (240 ml) whole wheat flour, any variety
- » 1 cup (240 ml) protein powder
- » 1 teaspoon baking powder
- » 1 teaspoon baking soda
- » ¼ teaspoon nutmeg
- » ½ teaspoon cinnamon
- » 1¼ cups (300 ml) unsweetened applesauce
- » ½ cup (120 ml) sucanat, either variety
- » 1 teaspoon vanilla
- » ½ cup (120 ml) raisins, dried cranberries, dried chopped apples or a mixture of all three

1. *Preheat oven: 275°F (140°C).*

2. *Combine first seven ingredients in a large mixing bowl. Combine applesauce, sucanat, and vanilla in small bowl and add to dry ingredients. Add dried fruit and mix well.*

3. *If mixture is too dry, then add more applesauce. Roll into small balls.*

4. *Place on cookie sheet and gently flatten with a fork.*

5. *Bake for 20-25 minutes. Serve.*

Makes 24 bars.

Cranberries

These shiny scarlet berries are grown in big sand bogs on low trailing vines. They are extensively cultivated in Massachusetts, Wisconsin, Washington, and Oregon. Harvested September through early November, the peak market period is around Thanksgiving and Christmas. Discard any cranberries that are discolored or shriveled. Cranberries can be refrigerated, tightly wrapped for at least two months, or frozen up to a year.

Wild Mushroom Oven Frittata

This rich, hearty frittata is perfect for a leisurely weekend brunch, or serve it for dinner with a mixed green salad and crusty bread.

- » 8 ounces (224 g) sliced wild mushrooms
- » ½ cup (120 ml) shallot (or onion)—chopped
- » 4 ounces (112 g) Boars Head Cajun Turkey—chopped
- » ½ teaspoon dried thyme
- » ½ teaspoon ground black pepper
- » 8 eggs
- » ½ cup (120 ml) heavy whipping cream or yo-cheese
- » 8 ounce (224 g) fontina cheese—shredded Italian cheese blend

1. *Preheat oven: 325°F (163°C).*

2. *In large skillet, cook mushrooms, shallot, turkey, thyme, and pepper over medium high heat until mushrooms are tender (about 8 minutes).*

3. *Cool completely.*

4. *In large bowl, whisk together eggs and cream. Stir in mushroom mixture and cheese. Pour into 9-inch deep-dish pie plate that has been greased. Bake until center is set, about 40-45 minutes. Cool slightly before cutting into wedges.*

Makes 8 servings.

 ## Shallots

Shallots come in a clove similar to garlic. Dry shallots will keep for months in a cool and dry location. Fresh shallots can be refrigerated for up to a week. When shopping, avoid those that are wrinkled, soft or sprouting. Shallots have a sweet and delicate flavor and can be used like other onions.

Yogurt

Without a yogurt maker

» 1 quart (.95 L) whole or 2 percent milk—raw milk is perfect

» 1-2 tablespoons plain yogurt or 1-2 tablespoons of commercial starter culture

1. *Warm up the milk in a sauce pan over medium-low heat until bubbles appear around the edge and steam rises from the surface. Pour the warm milk into a large bowl to cool until the temperature reaches 110 to 115 degrees (test the temperature by using a cooking thermometer), or until you can keep your index finger in the warm milk for 20 seconds. Put the starter in a small bowl, add some of the heated milk, and stir until well blended. Return the mixture to the large bowl a third at a time, making sure to stir and blend well after each addition. End with a final stir, making sure all is well blended. Cover with a heavy towel and keep in a warm place or oven 6-8 hours or overnight. (Placing a saucepan of hot water in the oven to raise the temperature will help if your home is not warm enough).*

2. *When set, cover the bowl with plastic wrap and refrigerate for 8 hours before serving. If thicker yogurt is desired, empty chilled yogurt in cheesecloth, suspend over a bowl, and drain or use a yogurt funnel.*

Yogurt

With a yogurt maker

» 1 quart (.95 L) whole or 2 percent milk—raw milk is perfect
» 1 tablespoon plain yogurt or 1 tablespoon of a commercial starter culture
» You can use a yogurt maker with cooking thermometer. The Donvier brand with eight jars is useful.

1. *Warm up the milk in a saucepan over medium-low heat until bubbles appear around the edge and steam rises from the surface. Remove the saucepan from heat and insert a thermometer stirrer. When the temperature reaches 110 to 115 degrees, add the starter to one of the jars. Add some of the heated milk and stir until well blended. Pour the mixture back into the saucepan, a little at a time, stirring well.*

2. *Fill all 8 jars, cover securely with lids, and place the jars into the "machine" which is a temperature controlled warmer and follow the cooking instructions. It will take 6-10 hours—easy to do overnight, depending on the tartness and firmness desired.*

3. *When done, store the jars in the refrigerator for a few hours before serving. You can keep the yogurt for up to 2 weeks in the fridge.*

Breads

Whole Grain
Goodness

History of White Flour

Many of us were enjoying bread freely until along comes the low carb diets giving bread a bad name. What is the real truth? Let's compare how the wheat grain (whole grain flour) contributes to excellent health, versus white flour contributing to problems.

The wheat kernel was created, as well as other grains, to be stored perfectly with lots of nutrients inside. Once the kernel is broken by milling, the nutrients begin to oxidize. Within about 72 hours, over 90% of all nutrients are virtually gone. The absence of these nutrients and the bulk of the fiber is what causes the suffering from many health problems, such as the ones listed on the Fiber Analysis.

When the wheat kernels are milled into white flour, the bran and the germ are removed. Only the endosperm remains in white flour. The chart shows how much nutrient value is lost. The removal of these nutrients allows the bleached white flour to be stored indefinitely.

Whole Wheat Flour	Loss in White Flour
Thiamine (B-1)	77%
Niacin (B-3)	81%
Pyridoxine (B-6)w	72%
Choline	30%
Folic acid and Riboflavin	67%
Pantothenic acid	50%
Vitamin E	86%
Chromium	40%
Manganese	86%

Selenium	16%
Zinc	98%
Iron	75%
Cobalt	89%
Calcium	60%
Sodium	78%
Potassium	77%
Magnesium	85%
Phosphorus	91%
Molybdenum	48%
Copper	68%
Fiber	89%

Vitamins B-1, B-2, B-3, iron, and folic acid are added to white flour in synthetic form by a process called enrichment.

Many of the foods we now eat for convenience are literally making us sick because they are devoid of the fiber and the nutrients that are essential to our health. Yet, life-giving whole foods are available. With the purchase of a grain mill and the baking of your own bread, your family will discover many positive results, including eliminating the craving for sweets and no more constipation (a very common problem—over 90% of Americans suffer from this inconvenience).

Once you decide to make your own bread and bread products for health benefits, the economics will be an added benefit. The initial investment of a grain mill and perhaps a Bosch mixer will soon be forgotten when you taste the homemade goodness of your own fresh bread. The cost of homemade bread will be $0.75-$1.00 per loaf. That is quite a savings, and the taste and health benefits just add to this blessing.

GLUTEN INTOLERANCE

Bread rises to the center with the health it provides, yet millions of people have a gluten intolerance (GI) inhibiting them from enjoying whole grain breads. Gluten is the protein found in wheat. This disease is a by-product of living in a culture where the predominant food is processed. Gluten intolerance is not a reflection of the Designer of bread but of the alteration of wheat.

For those who are gluten intolerant, the grains of choice would be corn, rice, soy, potato flour, hominy, buckwheat, millet, amaranth, quinoa and arrowroot. Some people with a mild case of GI can consume oats and oat bran.

A FIBER ANALYSIS

INSOLUABLE FIBERS	SOLUABLE FIBERS
Food Sources Bran of whole grains: wheat bran corn bran rice bran Legumes	**Food Sources** Oats (bran) Dried fruits Apples, pears (flesh) Membranes of oranges Most vegetables Seeds, Barley, Spelt
Assists digestive regularity contributing to the prevention and regulation of: Appendicitis Colon cancer Constipation Crohn's disease Diverticular disease Hemorrhoids Hiatal hernia Obesity Spastic colon Ulcerative colitis Varicose veins	Helps regulate appropriate blood sugar and cholesterol levels contributing to prevention and regulation of: Coronary heart disease Diabetes Gallstones High blood pressure Hypoglycemia
Cellulose is a form of fiber from the foods listed above that forms mucus in the intestine, destroying the parasite that causes irritable bowel syndrome.	Recent studies show that rice and barley bran lower cholesterol, perhaps not because of the fiber, but because of antioxidant properties in the oil of the grain.

GETTING STARTED MAKING BREAD

What you need to get started with mixer mixing:

- A good quality mixer such as a Bosch Universal even mixes up cookie dough. If you have a Kitchen Aid—only make 2 loaves at a time and let the machine rest because it is not designed to handle the 5 loaf recipe in this cookbook.
- A high quality electric grain mill such as the Nutrimill.
- 4 of the 8-inch waffle weave or stainless steel loaf pans (you can buy various sizes)
- Package of yeast—the vacuum-packed yeast is less expensive than the packets or bottles in your local grocery store. The vacuum-packed packages can be found online, (see resource section) at some Mediterranean stores, or some health food stores.
- Real Salt—this is the least processed brand of sea salt. There are lots of sea salt varieties in all stores so be choosy and select the highest quality. There are many trace minerals in Real Salt that are good for health.
- One dough scraper—makes it fun and easy to work with dough
- Heavy duty bread bags (washable, reusable)
- Wheat: Hard Red, Hard White, Soft White—pastry, other options could be Spelt, Kamut, etc.

What you need to get started with a bread machine:

- A high quality electric grain mill such as the Nutrimill
- A good quality bread machine such as the Zojuirishi (programmable horizontal loaf)
- Package of yeast
- Real Salt
- Heavy duty bread bags
- Wheat:
    Hard Red
    Hard White
    Soft White
    Other options could be Spelt, Kamut, etc.

What you need to get started with hand kneading:

- A high quality electric grain mill such as the Nutrimill
- Package of yeast
- Real Salt
- Heavy duty bread bags
- One dough scraper
- Wheat:
  - Hard Red
  - Hard White
  - Soft White
  - Other options could be Spelt, Kamut, etc.

The best places to find everything you need to make bread can be found on the Designed Healthy Living website. There are also References listed to call for assistance in making bread.

Store the fresh grains you purchase in a 5-gallon bucket sealed with a Gamma Lid. These two items will save your grain and your fingers each time you open the bucket. Both items can be purchased at bread suppliers on the internet and in some cities.

Denise's Soft and Satiny Dinner Rolls or Bread

"This recipe makes a velvety-smooth loaf of bread or soft and moist rolls. It has won many ribbons at our local 4-H fair and is my most requested recipe," Denise Fidler, owner of The Country Baker. www.countrybaker.com. Used with permission.

First: Using the Nutrimill, grind 12 cups of hard white whole wheat or have on hand, 5 pounds (2.3 kg) of flour. (18-22 cups/4.3-5.3 L). In Bosch Mixer bowl, place:

» 6 cups (1.4 L) really warm water (115-130 degrees)
» ½ cup (120 ml) dry milk powder or buttermilk powder
» ⅓ cup (75 ml) dry lecithin
» ¾ cup (180 ml) extra virgin olive oil or safflower oil
» 1¼ cups (300 ml) raw honey
» 1 tablespoon instant yeast
» 10 cups (2.4 l) of the flour

Then add:
» 3 tablespoons salt
» 3 tablespoons dough enhancer (or 2 vitamin C—crushed)
» ½ cup (120 ml) gluten

1. *Mix slightly on lowest speed then cover and let set for 10-15 minutes or longer. This is called sponging. Be careful, though, your dough may come up over the sides of your pan!*

1. *Add enough remaining flour to create a soft and slightly moist dough. The dough should clean away from the sides of the bowl. Knead 5-7 minutes in Bosch mixer on speed 1-2. For a more 'pronounced flavor,' you may cover and let rise until double and punch down before shaping.*

2. *Shape into rolls: Roll dough out into a rope and tie as for a knot, tucking the ends up in through the middle from the bottom.*

(Continued on next page...)

Denise's Soft and Satiny Dinner Rolls or Bread (continued)

3. *Shape into bread: Take dough out of Bosch bowl and shape into a neat 'log'.*

4. *Divide dough into about 4 equal pieces that will fit snugly into the 8 inch greased Norpro 1½# pans. Tuck each piece of dough into the pan, squeezing and tucking down toward the bottom. The pans should each be filled about $^2/_3$ of the way.*

5. *Cover and let rise until double in a warm, draft-free place. This should take anywhere from 20-40 minutes. I preheat my oven and place the loaves on top while it is preheating. Some people prefer to set the loaves in a slightly preheated oven that has been turned off and then turned back on again after about 20 minutes.*

6. *If desired, beat 1 egg or egg white with a splash of water and brush onto loaves or rolls. Sprinkle with oat, rye, or whole grain flakes. Sesame or poppy seeds work well, too. This makes a beautiful presentation and the flakes or seeds add a delicious toasted flavor to the bread.*

7. *Bake at 350°F (180°C) for 20-25 minutes for rolls and 30-35 minutes for bread. Recipe makes approximately 12-15 dozen rolls or four 8-inch loaves of bread that freeze well.*

Israelite Unleavened Bread

Adapted from *Food at the Time of the Bible*, by Miriam Feinberg Vamosh

» 2 cups (470 ml) whole wheat bread—hard white or spelt
» ¾ cup (180 ml) cold water
» 2 tablespoons olive oil
» 1 teaspoon salt
» ½ medium onion—chopped finely
» 1 garlic clove—minced

1. Preheat oven 500°F (260°C).

2. Combine all ingredients with the water to form a dough and knead for 3 minutes.

3. Divide into 8 balls. Flatten each into a thin round and prick with a fork.

4. Bake on a greased cookie sheet for 10 minutes in oven.

Flavorful Variations

* Try this for your next Passover meal or Lord's Supper observance.
* Top with hummus and chopped fresh vegetables for a perfect lunch treat.
* Top with cheese and peppers for an appetizer, broil to melt cheese.
* Use as a crust for personal pizzas.

Olive Oil Dipping Sauce

» ½ cup (120 ml) extra virgin olive oil
» ¼ teaspoon salt
» 5 garlic cloves—minced
» 2 teaspoons Italian seasoning

1. Mix all ingredients together. Store in refrigerator and bring to room temperature before serving.

Whole Wheat Honey Bread (5 loaves)

If you want a bread that is a little moist and sweet, then this version may suite your taste.

- » Mill 13 cups (3.1 L) of grain—yields 19-21 cups (4.6-5.0 L) of flour
- » 6 cups (1.4 L) warm water
- » ⅔ cup (150 ml) olive oil
- » 1⅓ (315 ml) cup honey
- » 4 eggs
- » 4 tablespoons yeast
- » 2 tablespoons dough enhancer, opt.
- » 4 tablespoons lecithin, opt.
- » 10 cups (2.4 L) flour

Then add:
- » 1½ tablespoons gluten, opt.
- » 2 tablespoons salt
- » 10-11 cups (2.4—2.7 L) of flour

1. *Mix the above ingredients in the Bosch mixer and let sponge for 15 minutes. Sponging will allow the yeast to ferment and grow. This is sometimes referred to as testing the yeast.*

2. *Preheat oven: 350°F (180°C).*

3. *Mix in gluten, salt, and flour until the dough begins to pull away from the sides of the machine. Then let the machine knead the dough for 5-7 minutes on low speed. Take dough out and shape into the loaf pans. Let rise for 30 minutes and bake for 27 minutes.*

For more information on mixing this bread, refer to the instructions in "Denise's Soft and Satiny Bread" in the Bosch mixer.

 Yeast

Hot water kills yeast. Warm water is best when making yeast breads. Test the water on your forearm. It should not feel too hot or cold.

Buy yeast in a vacuum-packed package rather than the small packets or glass bottles in your local grocery store. This saves money and can be stored in mason jars in the refrigerator for freshness.

Whole Wheat Honey Bread

One 2 pound (908 g) loaf

- » 1½ cups (360 ml) hot water
- » ⅓ cup (75 ml) olive oil
- » ⅓ cup (75 ml) honey—less is ok
- » 5 cups (1.2 L) whole wheat flour—hard red or hard white
- » 2 teaspoons salt
- » 2 tablespoons lecithin—optional
- » 2 tablespoons ground flax seed—optional
- » 1 egg
- » 1 tablespoon yeast

1. *Place ingredients in your bread machine in the order listed. Make sure paddles are in place first. Bake on desired setting.*

My family's favorite bread recipe can be used for buns and rolls.

Makes 20 rolls.

Bread Machine: Set the bread machine on dough cycle. Then when the cycle is finished take the dough out of the bread machine and shape it into a loaf. If the dough is a little sticky, knead a small amount of flour into it as you shape it.
Place in a greased loaf pan. Let rise for approximately 40 minutes. Bake at 350°F (180°C) for 27 minutes. Makes 2, one pound (454 g) loaves or 1, two pound (908 g) loaf.

I use the dough cycle *and* my oven because it comes out looking like a normal loaf of bread, especially since my bread machine is a vertical loaf pan which causes the bread to be a little heavier. The Zojurishi Bread machine makes a nice horizontal loaf. Look for it at www.countrybaker.com. Mention Designed Healthy Living for a special savings.

Hand Kneading

The Bosch and other bread machines are designed to develop the gluten in the bread to make a soft and fluffy loaf of whole wheat bread. Hand kneading can produce the same result, but requires more effort and time.

(Continued on next page…)

Hand Kneading (continued)

Start with the ingredients for the Whole Wheat Honey Bread—One 2 pound (908 g) loaf. Add half of the flour and all of the other ingredients except salt. Allow to sponge for 30-45 minutes. Then continue to mix in the remaining flour and salt with a wooden spoon until you have a mass of dough that is no longer clinging to the sides of the bowl. Flip out on the counter or table top and start the kneading process.

Begin by pushing away and pulling forward the dough and then give it a ¼ turn and push and pull again. Continue this process until the dough is smooth and satiny. This could take 10-30 minutes depending on the recipe and how vigorous a kneader you are. When you are pushing and pulling, be sure to pull the dough up and over from front to back and back to front.

To test for gluten development, break off a tennis ball-sized piece of dough and stretch it really thin. If you get windows or parts of the dough that you can see through, then you have successfully developed the gluten. This will be similar to a consistency of chewed bubble gum. If it just breaks apart in your hands then it's necessary to continue kneading a bit longer until the dough is soft and stretchy. It should be smooth and have a light and springy texture to it. You may cover the dough in a greased bowl and let it rise until doubled and punch down (this process creates a finer texture and more pronounced flavor), or you can shape and bake it. Information gathered from *Wildflour,* by Denise Fidler.

Spinach-Cheese French Bread

» 1 small onion—chopped
» 2 tablespoons butter
» 1 package 10 ounce (280g) frozen chopped spinach, thawed and squeezed dry—or fresh spinach cooked and chopped
» 1 cup (240 ml) mozzarella cheese, shredded—Farmers cheese works well
» 1 cup (240 ml) shredded cheddar cheese
» 1 cup (240 ml) chopped fresh mushrooms
» ⅛ teaspoon salt
» ⅛ teaspoon pepper
» ⅛ teaspoon hot pepper sauce—optional
» 1 loaf French bread halved lengthwise
» ½ cup (120 ml) parmesan cheese

1. *Preheat oven: 350°F (180°C).*

2. *In large skillet, sauté onion in butter until tender. Remove from heat. Stir in spinach, cheeses, mushrooms, salt, pepper and hot pepper sauce.*

3. *Spoon onto bread halves.*

4. *Place on an ungreased baking sheet. Sprinkle with Parmesan Cheese.*

5. *Bake for 10-15 minutes or until cheese is melted.*

Spinach-Cheese Stromboli

Follow step 1 above for sautéing onions and adding spinach, cheese, mushrooms, and seasonings. Roll out dough into a rectangle and spoon the spinach cheese mixture to cover ⅔ of the dough. Then the dough can be rolled up like a sleeping bag, or the edges can be rolled and made into an edge and baked like a pizza. Bake 425°F (180°C) for 15 minutes.

Ranch Pizza Pinwheels

Pizza crust dough
- » ¼ cup (60 ml) prepared ranch salad dressing
- » ½ cup (120 ml) shredded Colby Monterey Jack cheese—or cheese of your choice
- » ½ cup (120 ml) diced meat—your choice
- » ¼ cup (60 ml) chopped green onions

1. *Preheat oven: 425°F (220°C).*

2. *On a lightly floured surface, roll pizza dough into a 12 inch x 10 inch rectangle. Spread ranch dressing evenly to within ¼ of edges. Sprinkle with cheese, meat, and onions. Roll up jelly-roll style, starting with long side.*

3. *Cut into 1 inch slices. Place cut side down on a greased baking sheet.*

4. *Bake for 10-13 minutes or until lightly browned.*

Serve warm with pizza sauce or additional ranch dressing if desired. Refrigerate leftovers.

❧ *Ranch Dressing*

Ranch Dressing can be made using the recipe in this book for a more flavorful, healthful contribution to this recipe.

Italian Bread

- » Italian Seasoning
- » Garlic powder
- » Red onions—thinly sliced
- » Cheese
- » Round pan—cake pan for baking
- » Bread dough—for one pound (454 g) loaf

1. Place the dough on a round cheese cake or plain round cake pan lightly oiled.

2. As it rises, add Italian seasoning, a bit of garlic powder plus thinly sliced onions on top. Red onions make it look very fancy, like Panera's Foccaccia bread. Cheese could be added also.

3. A Christmas bread could also have red and green peppers on top.

4. Cook as directed for bread.

Make Your Own Italian Seasoning

A favorite spice blend to keep on hand can be easy to make your self in case you run out. Mix 2 tablespoons of each of these spices; basil, marjoram, oregano, rosemary, and thyme, and store in an air tight container.

Pizza Dough

- » 1½ cups (360 ml) warm water
- » 1 tablespoon yeast
- » 1 egg
- » ½ teaspoon salt
- » 1 tablespoon sucanat with honey
- » 4 cups (960 ml) whole wheat flour—hard white
- » ½ teaspoon garlic seasoning or to taste (optional)
- » ½ teaspoon Italian seasoning or to taste (optional)

1. *Preheat oven: 375°F (190°C).*

2. *Mix in order and knead. Let rise until doubled. Punch dough down. Divide dough into 2 pieces.*

3. *Oil pizza pans and spread out dough.*

Dough makes 2 pizzas.

Sauce

6 ounce (168 g) tomato paste, 8 ounce (224 g) tomato sauce, ½ teaspoon, oregano, ½ teaspoon basil, 1 teaspoon Italian seasoning, ½ teaspoon onion salt, ½ teaspoon celery salt. Mix to taste and consistency desired. Spread on dough. Top with favorite toppings. Sprinkle Italian seasoning on top of the cheeses if desired. Bake for 20 minutes.

 ## Freezing pizza dough

Should you freeze the pizza dough unbaked or after it has been baked? It works well either way, though baked crusts take up more room than unbaked dough. Place your frozen dough on the counter to thaw in the morning and let come to room temperature while still wrapped. The dough that has been frozen and thawed has a nice "yeasty" smell and tastes somewhat like sourdough. It may not be as light as made up fresh, but the flavor is still good.

Another good idea is to use the large round Tupperware container (cake or cupcake carrier). Roll out the crust, being sure to fit the crust size into the Tupperware container. Bake the crust for about 8-10 minutes, cool and wrap well before freezing. The container holds about 2-3 crusts.

Poppy Seed Rolls

» 1 egg
» 1 tablespoon water
» 1½ cups (360 ml) yogurt—unsweetened
» 4 tablespoon olive oil
» 2½ cups (590 ml) soft wheat flour
» 2 tablespoon sucanat honey
» 1 tablespoon baking powder
» 1 teaspoon salt
» 1 teaspoon poppy seeds

1. *Mix together the egg and water. Set aside for later.*

2. *Whip the yogurt and olive oil to a smooth consistency. Sift together flour, sucanat, salt, and baking powder. Make a well and pour the yogurt-oil mixture into the center. Stir until it forms a soft ball. Then knead on a floured surface until it no longer sticks and has a smooth consistency.*

3. *Preheat the oven to 400°F (200°C).*

4. *Make 12 round rolls and put on a baking sheet. Brush with egg-water mixture and sprinkle with seeds. Using a sharp knife, make a cross on top of each roll. Bake in the preheated oven for 30 minutes or until the rolls are golden.*

Rolls are good warm, but you can serve them at room temperature.

Poppy Seeds

Poppy Seeds are a classic addition to buttered egg noodles, fruit salad dressings, and fragrant yeast breads. Poppy Seeds add nutty flavor and texture to cookies, cakes, breads, strudels, pastry crusts, and pancake and waffle batters. Because of their high oil content, all poppy seeds are prone to rancidity and should be stored airtight in the refrigerator for up to 6 months. (It is true that poppy seeds can give a false positive for drug screening and show up as opiates.)

Cream Cheese Biscuits

- » 2 cups (470 ml) whole wheat flour—hard white
- » 1 tablespoon baking powder
- » ¾ teaspoon salt
- » 3 ounce (84 g) cream cheese
- » ½ stick butter
- » ⅔ cup (150 ml) buttermilk

1. *Preheat oven: 450°F (230°C).*

2. *Mix together dry ingredients. Cut in cream cheese and butter. Make a well in the center of the dry ingredients; pour in milk. Mix together to form a ball.*

3. *Turn out onto floured surface and knead 10-12 times. Roll out to ½ inch thickness and cut into rounds. Bake 10-12 minutes. For a more tender biscuit, place rounds on a cookie sheet with sides touching.*

Makes 12 biscuits.

Flavorful Variations

* Fresh or dried herbs can be added to this recipe for a different taste that will be very pleasing. Regular or almond milk can also be used instead of buttermilk.

Cinnamon Raisin Biscuits

Using the recipe above, add 3 tablespoons of sucanat, 1 tablespoon cinnamon, and ¼ cup (60 ml) raisins. Bake as directed. These are very soft and creamy.

Applesauce Muffins

» 1 stick butter
» ⅓ cup (75 ml) olive oil or safflower oil
» 2 cups (470 ml) sucanat—either variety
» 2 eggs
» 1 teaspoon vanilla
» 2 teaspoons baking soda
» 2 cups (470 ml) applesauce
» 4 cups (960 ml) whole wheat flour—soft white pastry
» 2 teaspoons cinnamon
» ¾ teaspoon allspice
» ¾ teaspoon cloves

1. *Preheat oven: 375°F (190°C).*

2. *Cream the first 5 ingredients. Add baking soda to applesauce. Combine with creamed ingredients. Add dry ingredients. Bake for approximately 20 minutes.*

Makes 12 muffins.

 ### Applesauce

Making your own applesauce is worth the time and effort. Find your favorite apple—mine are Jonagold and Pink Lady. After picking or purchasing your apples, use a good vegetable wash (organic) to clean off all pesticides. Then peel, core, and slice them into a crock pot. Add ½ cup sucanat or less to a full crock pot. Let cook for several hours on high. Use a potato masher to puree the apples as they get tender. Add cinnamon at the end of the cooking. The applesauce is done when it has the flavor and texture you prefer.

Orange Carrot Muffins

» ⅓ cup (75 ml) butter
» ½ cup (120 ml) sucanat
» 2 eggs
» 1¾ cups (420 ml) whole wheat flour—soft white pastry or hard white
» 1 teaspoon baking soda
» 1 teaspoon baking powder
» ⅛ teaspoon nutmeg
» ⅛ teaspoon cloves
» ½ cup (120 ml) orange juice
» 2 cups (470 ml) shredded carrots

1. *Preheat oven: 350°F (180°C).*

2. *In a large mixing bowl, cream butter and sucanat. Add eggs and beat well.*

3. *Combine the flour, baking soda, baking powder, nutmeg, and cloves in separate bowl.*

4. *Add to creamed mixture alternating with orange juice. Fold in carrots.*

5. *Fill greased muffin cups ¾ full. Bake for 18-22 minutes.*

Flavorful Variations

* Add ¾ cup (180 ml) of cooked apples in place of orange juice

Hints for oiling and dusting your bread and muffin pans

Dust a bread pan or work surface with flour by filling a large empty glass salt shaker with flour.

Use olive oil for pans to add a little nutrition rather than spray bottles with propellant. Pour a little oil in the pans and coat using a paper towel. Then pour a drop or two of liquid lecithin (found at good health food stores) in the oiled pan and spread this around using the same paper towel. The lecithin will make the bread come out beautifully. Lecithin is very good for your health, or you can make your own olive oil and lecithin mixture.

Recipe for olive oil and lecithin: ⅔ cup (150 ml) olive oil, ⅓ (75 ml) cup lecithin. Mix together. Store in glass container in refrigerator.

Buckwheat Corn Muffins

- » 1 cup (240 ml) buckwheat flour
- » ½ cup (120 ml) cornmeal—whole grain
- » 2½ teaspoons baking powder
- » ½ teaspoon salt
- » ¼ cup (60 ml) sucanat with honey or 1 mashed banana
- » 2 eggs
- » 1¼ cups (300 ml) buttermilk
- » ¼ cup (60 ml) oil

1. *Preheat oven: 375°F (190°C).*

2. *Mix dry ingredients. Mix liquid ingredients and combine. Fill oiled muffin cups. Bake approximately 12 minutes. Check top of muffins for doneness.*

Makes 12 muffins.

Flavorful Variations

* Add 1 cup (240 ml) pumpkin and 2 tablespoons of cinnamon, pecans, or walnuts.
* Add fruit: blueberries, peaches, strawberries, etc.

Note: Fresh milled corn and buckwheat will taste best.

Buckwheat

While many people think buckwheat is a cereal grain, it is actually a fruit seed that is related to rhubarb and sorrel, making it a suitable substitute for grains for people who are sensitive to wheat or other grains that contain protein glutens. Buckwheat flowers are very fragrant and are attractive to bees that use them to produce a special, strong flavored, dark honey.

The health benefits of buckwheat*:
- Linked to lowered risk of developing high cholesterol and high blood pressure
- Better blood sugar control and a lowered risk of diabetes
- Helps prevent gallstones
- Protective against breast cancer

*www.whfoods.com

Cinnamon Rhubarb Muffins

- » 1½ cups (360 ml) whole wheat flour
- » ½ cup (120 ml) plus 1 tablespoon sucanat with honey
- » 2 teaspoon baking powder
- » 1¼ teaspoon cinnamon
- » ¼ teaspoon salt
- » 1 egg
- » ⅔ cup (150 ml) buttermilk
- » ¼ cup (60 ml) butter—melted
- » ½ cup (120 ml) chopped fresh or frozen rhubarb—thawed and drained
- » ¼ cup (60 ml) preserves: peach, strawberry, or apple

1. *Preheat oven: 400°F (200°C).*

2. *In a bowl, combine flour, ½ cup sucanat, baking powder, 1-teaspoon cinnamon and salt. Combine egg, buttermilk, and butter in separate bowl. Stir into dry ingredients just until moistened. Spoon 1 tablespoon of batter into 9 greased muffin cups. Combine rhubarb and preserves in a bowl. Place 1 tablespoon of mixture in the center of each cup (do not spread). Top with remaining batter. Combine remaining sucanat and cinnamon together. Sprinkle over batter. Bake for 20 minutes or until top of muffin springs back when touched in the center.*

Makes 9 muffins. (In a hurry—mix the rhubarb and preserves in batter.)

 ## Whole Wheat Flours—Which one to use?

An easy way to remember which flour or grain to use while baking and cooking:
Hard red and hard white are usually used when yeast is in the recipe. Hard Red is a little more flavorful or nutty tasting.
Soft White or Pastry flour is typically used when no yeast is in the recipe.
Muffins are an exception to the rule and can use any flour.

Oat Flour Muffins

- » 2 cups (470 ml) oat flour—Arrowhead is good, or make your own by placing dry old-fashioned oats in a blender
- » 1 tablespoon baking powder
- » 1 teaspoon salt
- » ⅓ cup (75 ml) honey
- » 1 teaspoon vanilla
- » 1 cup (240 ml) raisins
- » 2 tablespoons olive oil
- » ⅔ cup (150 ml) buttermilk
- » 2 eggs

1. Preheat oven: 375°F (190°C).

2. Stir together dry ingredients, pressing out any lumps. Mix liquids and raisins together, and then add to dry mix, stirring lightly. Let sit a couple minutes and stir again.

3. Pour into lightly-greased muffin tins.

4. Bake for 15-20 minutes for full size muffins.

Makes 12 muffins.

Muffins freeze well if you use oil. You can also add a little pumpkin and raisins to many of these recipes.

 **Buttermilk**

If you are caught without any buttermilk you can make it easily by using 1 cup of skim milk and a tablespoon of lemon juice. Using a tablespoon of cream of tartar will work as well, and this will not be quite as acidic.

Morning Glory Muffins

- » 1¼ cups (300 ml) whole wheat flour—hard red
- » 1¼ cups (300 ml) whole wheat four—soft white pastry
- » 1 cup (240 ml) sucanat—either variety
- » 2 teaspoons baking soda
- » 2 teaspoons cinnamon—ground
- » ½ teaspoon salt
- » 2 cups (470 ml) carrots—shredded
- » 1 cup (240 ml) apple—chopped
- » ¾ cup (180 ml) raisins
- » ⅓ cup (75 ml) pecans—chopped
- » 8 ounce (224 g) pineapple—crushed, drained
- » ¼ cup (60 ml) coconut—unsweetened
- » ⅓ cup (75 ml) olive oil
- » ⅓ cup (75 ml) apple butter
- » 2 teaspoons vanilla
- » 2 eggs
- » 2 egg whites

1. *Preheat oven: 350°F (180°C).*

2. *Combine flours, sucanat, soda, cinnamon, and salt in large bowl. Stir in carrot, apple, raisins, pecans, pineapple, and coconut. Make a well in center of mixture. Combine oil and next four ingredients, stir in with a whisk. Add oil mixture to flour mixture, stirring until moist. Spoon batter into 24 muffin cups sprayed with oil.*

3. *Bake for approximately 20-25 minutes, testing for doneness.*

Remove and let cool on wire rack. Makes 24 muffins.

Pumpkin Chocolate Chip Muffins

- » 1 cup (240 ml) whole wheat flour—hard white
- » ⅔ cup whole wheat flour—hard red
- » 1 cup (240 ml) sucanat with honey
- » 1 teaspoon pumpkin pie spice
- » 1 teaspoon cinnamon
- » 1 teaspoon baking soda
- » ¼ teaspoon baking powder
- » ¼ teaspoon salt
- » 2 large eggs
- » ⅓ cup (75 ml) pumpkin
- » 1 cup (240 ml) mini chocolate chips
- » ⅓ cup olive oil

1. *Preheat oven: 350°F (180°C).*

2. *Mix dry ingredients together well. Add remaining ingredients and mix well until just moistened. Spoon into greased muffin tins.*

3. *Bake for 20-25 minutes for standard size muffins. Bake 10-15 minutes for mini muffins.*

Makes 12 muffins or 36 mini muffins.

 Crunchy Topping for Muffins

For a quick, low-fat crunchy topping for muffins, sprinkle the tops with granola (coarse or ground in your blender) before baking. See granola recipe.

Zucchini Bread/Muffins

- » 3 eggs—beaten
- » ½ cup (120 ml) oil
- » ¾ cup (470 ml) sucanat
- » 1 teaspoon vanilla
- » 3 cups (720 ml) whole wheat flour—soft white
- » 2 teaspoons cinnamon
- » 1 teaspoon baking soda
- » 1½ teaspoons baking powder
- » 3 cups (720 ml) zucchini—coarsely chopped
- » 1 teaspoon salt

1. *Preheat oven: 350°F (180°C).*

2. *Combine eggs, oil, vanilla, and sucanat in mixing bowl. In separate bowl combine flour, cinnamon, salt, baking soda, and baking powder. Add to mixing bowl ingredients, mix well. Add zucchini, mix well. Pour into baking dishes.*

3. *Top with nuts, sucanat and cinnamon if desired.*

4. *For loaves of bread, bake for one hour. For muffins, bake for approximately 15 minutes.*

Makes 2 loaves of bead, 12 regular muffins or 48 mini muffins.

≋ *Flavorful Variations*

* Substitute applesauce or pumpkin puree for oil. Add ½ cup chopped nuts.

Barley Cakes

- » 1½ cups (360 ml) barley flour
- » ½ cup (120 ml) whole wheat flour—hard white
- » ¼ teaspoon salt
- » 1 cup (240 ml) milk
- » 1 egg
- » 1 cup (240 ml) honey

1. Preheat oven to 425°F (220°C).

2. Mix flours and salt. Add in the milk and egg, stirring constantly. Then add the honey. Drop spoonfuls of the mixture on a greased baking tray, leaving space for the cakes to spread.

3. Bake 10-15 minutes, until done.

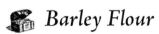 **Barley Flour**

Barley flour can be made by milling your own barley. These seeds can be found from several co-ops where wheat is supplied. The barley cakes are surprisingly very tasty.

Banana Loaf

- » ½ cup (120 ml) olive oil
- » 1½ cups (360 ml) sucanat with honey or ½ cup (120 ml) honey
- » 2 eggs
- » 1 teaspoon vanilla
- » 2 cups (470 ml) whole wheat flour—soft white pastry
- » ½ teaspoon salt
- » ½ cup (120 ml) ground flax seed—optional
- » ½ teaspoon baking powder
- » ¾ teaspoon baking soda
- » 1 cup (240 ml) chopped nuts
- » 1 cup (240 ml) banana—mashed
- » ¼ cup (60 ml) yogurt
- » ½ cup (120 ml) nuts

1. Preheat oven: 325°F (163°C).

2. Cream together oil and add sucanat, eggs, vanilla. Combine dry ingredients and add to liquid mixture. Add mashed bananas, yogurt and nuts. Stir lightly. Grease 1 large or 2 small loaf pans or 1 Bundt pan.

3. Bake approximately 40 minutes.

Flavorful Variations

* Olive oil may be replaced with ½ cup (120 ml) yogurt, making it a total of ¾ cup (180 ml) yogurt.
* Olive oil may also be replaced with pureed pumpkin, equal amounts.
* One stick of organic butter may be substituted for both olive oil and yogurt.
* Nuts can be replaced with mini chocolate chips.

Boston Brown Bread

Surprisingly tasty bread. A family heirloom keepsake.

- » 1½ cup (120 ml) water—boiling
- » 1 cup (240 ml) raisins
- » 2 teaspoons baking soda
- » 3 tablespoons butter
- » 1½ cup (120 ml) sucanat—natural
- » ½ cup (120 ml) molasses
- » 2 eggs
- » 1 teaspoon vanilla
- » 4 cups whole wheat flour—hard white
- » 1 teaspoon salt
- » 2 teaspoons cinnamon
- » ½ teaspoon nutmeg
- » 1 cup (240 ml) nuts—chopped

1. Preheat oven: 350°F (180°C).

2. Combine boiling water, raisins and baking soda. Let stand until cool. Cream butter, sucanat, molasses, eggs, and vanilla. Add flour, salt, cinnamon, and nutmeg.

3. Drain water from raisin mixture, reserving liquid. Add water to flour mixture. Gently stir in raisins and nuts.

4. Bake in 2 greased loaf pans for 1 hour.

Great for potlucks or to take to work and leave in the break room for everyone to nibble on.

My grandmother used to bake this bread in coffee cans. She would add a festive ribbon for family Christmas gifts.

Pumpkin Bread

- » 3 cups (720 ml) whole wheat flour—soft white pastry
- » 1 teaspoon salt
- » 3 teaspoons cinnamon
- » 2 teaspoons baking soda
- » 3 teaspoons nutmeg
- » ½ teaspoon ginger
- » 3 cups (720 ml) sucanat or 1½ cup (360 ml) honey
- » ⅓ cup (75 ml) olive oil
- » ⅔ cup (150 ml) water
- » 2 cups (470 ml) canned pumpkin or strained fresh pumpkin
- » ½ cup (120 ml) applesauce
- » 4 eggs
- » Nuts and dates—optional

1. *Preheat oven: 350°F (180°C).*

2. *Mix the dry ingredients well. Add the remaining ingredients.*

3. *Pour into loaf pans.*

4. *Bake for 1 hour. Store in refrigerator or freezer.*

Makes 3 loaves.

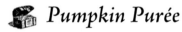 *Pumpkin Purée*

Pumpkin pie purée can be made in your very own kitchen; no longer the need to buy canned pumpkin. The fresh taste will amaze you. Find a pie pumpkin since it is typically sweeter and a finer texture than the Jack-O-Lantern variety. Cut the pumpkin in half and remove the seeds and strings. Then cut the pumpkin in large chunks and place on a baking sheet with one inch of water in the pan. Bake at 350 degrees F (200 C) for 45 minutes to one hour. Add more water if necessary to prevent drying out. The pumpkin needs to be fork tender. Remove from oven, allow to cool. When cool to touch remove the outer skins and place pumpkin in blender. Blend until smooth. Freeze in 2 cup (480 ml) containers.

Raspberry Streusel Bread

Topping:
- » ⅓ cup (75 ml) sucanat with honey
- » ¼ cup (60 ml) whole wheat flour
- » ¼ cup (60 ml) chopped pecans
- » 2 tablespoons butter—melted

Bread:
- » 1½ cups (360 ml) whole wheat flour—hard white or soft white pastry
- » ⅔ cup (150 ml) sucanat with honey
- » 2 teaspoons baking powder
- » ½ teaspoon salt
- » ½ cup (120 ml) milk (regular, soy, rice, almond or buttermilk)
- » 1 egg
- » 1 teaspoon vanilla
- » 1 cup (240 ml) unsweetened raspberries—fresh or thawed.

1. *Preheat oven: 400°F (200°C).*

2. *In small bowl, stir together topping ingredients until crumbly, set aside. In large mixing bowl, stir together flour, sucanat, baking powder, and salt. In small bowl stir together milk, egg, and vanilla. Pour into flour mixture. Stir just until dry ingredients are moistened.*

3. *Fold in thawed raspberries. Spoon batter into oiled and floured bread pan (1 large or 2 mini loaf pans) filling ⅔ full. Top each with about 4 heaping tablespoons of the topping mixture.*

4. *Bake for 35–40 minutes, or until a wooden pick inserted in center comes out clean. Cool slightly on wire rack.*

How to Alter Your Favorite Bread Recipes

Most of your favorite bread recipes can be made more healthful just by switching the ingredients. Milling your own wheat will add a lot of vitamins and fiber to every recipe. Keep a variety of grains on hand for selection. Change your current sugar or sugar substitute to Sucanat, Savannah Gold Crystals, or sucanat with honey. These dried sugar cane source sweeteners give you a delicious taste without the empty calorie, bleached white sugar. If your breads or muffins don't rise well, then add 1 teaspoon of baking powder or gluten.

Rice Bread

A light, gluten-free bread.

- » 3 eggs
- » ¼ cup (60 ml) milk or non fat dairy substitute
- » 4 tablespoons oil
- » 1 teaspoon vinegar
- » 1 tablespoon molasses or honey
- » 1½ cups (360 ml) water
- » 1½ cups (360 ml) milled brown rice flour
- » 1½ cups (360 ml) milled white rice flour
- » 1 tablespoon xanthan gum
- » 1 teaspoon salt
- » ⅓ cup (75 ml) sucanat with honey
- » 1 teaspoon unflavored gelatin
- » 2¼ teaspoons rapid rise yeast

1. *Place liquid ingredients in bread machine first, followed by dry ingredients. Begin cycle.*

Makes 1½ pound (227 g) loaf.

Note: This bread may be good for those suffering from Celiac or Candida disease.

Brown Rice Flour

Brown rice is a rich source of B vitamins, calcium and iron. It makes great pancakes and lightens up whole wheat flour recipes. Make your own in a Bosch mixer or Vita Mix Blender.

Xanthan Gum

Xanthan Gum is used by people who are allergic to gluten to add volume and viscosity to bread and other gluten-free baked goods. It is made from a tiny microorganism called Xanthomonas campestris and is a natural carbohydrate. Xanthan Gum helps replace the gluten in a recipe and aids in binding and thickening recipes. It is an essential ingredient in gluten-free baking.

Strawberry Nut Bread

» 3 cups (720 ml) whole wheat flour—hard white
» 1 teaspoon baking soda
» 1 teaspoon salt
» 2 teaspoon cinnamon
» 3 eggs—beaten
» 1¼ cups (300 ml) olive oil
» 1 cup (240 ml) honey
» 1¼ cups (300 ml) nuts—walnut, pecan
» 2 cups (470 ml) strawberries—fresh or frozen, drained and sliced

1. *Preheat oven: 350°F (180°C).*

2. *Combine dry ingredients. Beat eggs with the oil and add honey. Blend dry ingredients with liquid. Stir in thawed strawberries and nuts.*

3. *Spoon into 2 large or 3 small greased and floured loaf pans.*

4. *Bake approximately 50-60 minutes.*

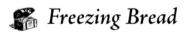 ## Freezing Bread

Most breads freeze beautifully. So if you are cooking for a small family and having a "baking" day—you can freeze a ½ loaf or a full loaf for later. Bread bags from Country Baker work well for this. Use the bread within one month.

Hawaiian Bread

- » ⅓ cup (75 ml) canned pineapple chunks—drained
- » 3 tablespoons buttermilk
- » 2 tablespoons reserved pineapple juice
- » 1½ teaspoons active dry yeast
- » 1 egg
- » ⅓ cup (75 ml) sliced very ripe banana
- » 2⅓ cups (555 ml) whole wheat flour
- » 1 teaspoon salt
- » 3 tablespoons butter
- » 1 tablespoon sucanat
- » ⅓ cup (75 ml) shredded coconut
- » ¼ cup (60 ml) chopped macadamia nuts

1. *Bread Machine: Put all ingredients into bread machine or follow your user's manual.*

2. *Select correct bread cycle and crust color, then press start.*

3. *Hand mixing: Combine all ingredients in order listed. Mix well. Put into greased loaf pan. Bake at 350 F for 25 minutes. Insert a knife—if it comes out clean the bread is done. If not, add 5 minutes and repeat till done.*

 Homemade bread crumbs

Start with 3-day-old sliced bread and place it in the oven until lightly toasted. Put bread in blender or food processor to make crumbs. Keep bread crumbs in the refrigerator for freshness.

Vegetables

From the Ground Up

Getting the Most from Your Fruits and Vegetables

Purchasing—Fresh is best. Purchasing fruits and vegetables in season will yield greater health rewards with higher nutritional value. Delight yourself in the 150 varieties of vegetables. Fresh produce should be purchased at a farmers market, private stand, or co-op. Grocery stores are getting into the 'local' scene, but the food can still come from at least 100 miles away and many times as much as 500 miles away.

Frozen is second best, especially if it was frozen after just being picked out of your garden.

Canned is the least nutritious. Use canned vegetables and fruits as your last resort and not on a continual basis, because you are missing out on the nutrients.

Storage—Most fruits and vegetables should be stored unwashed. Washing encourages bacteria and speeds deterioration. Wash fresh produce immediately before using with a high quality organic cleaner. Once the food is washed, peeled, or broken apart, store it in a container (glass is best), or in vegetable bags, and place in refrigerator.

Juice—Look for organic juices that are not from concentrate and contain purified water. No sugar or sugar substitutes should be added to the juice. Juice should be processed from American fruit and vegetables, i.e. Florida OJ.

Adding fruit and vegetables into the diet:
1. Add dried fruits to oatmeal or on top of cereal.
2. Combine dried fruits and nuts for a tasty snack.

3. Put sliced zucchini or cucumbers on sandwiches, along with lettuce and tomato.
4. Top meat or potatoes with fresh homemade salsa.
5. Purée fresh fruit to make sauce for meat, poultry, pancakes, waffles, or French toast. Add chopped apples or grapes to chicken or tuna salad.
7. Blend raw or cooked carrots into fruit smoothies.
8. Add new fruits to salads.
9. Add fresh vegetables to homemade pizza.

How Does Your Garden Grow?

Terms to help you understand:

Sustainable—The aim of sustainable agriculture is to be profitable and meet human consumption needs while caring for the environment—the land God gave us. Sustainable agriculture also addresses the quality of life for farm workers and communications.

Organic—The USDA defines organic as food produced using sustainable agriculture practices with no synthetic fertilizers, conventional pesticides, or bioengineering. Organic animal products come from animals given no antibiotics or growth hormones. Look for the USDA's "certified organic" seal, which indicates the item is made with at least 95% organic ingredients.

Natural—The FDA has not established a formal definition for the term "natural" but it does not object to the use of the term on product labels as long as the product contains no added color, artificial flavors, or synthetic substances. It says little about how the ingredients used to make the item should be grown or produced.

Local—This loose, unregulated term indicates an item was grown within a specific radius (typically no more than 100 miles). Buying locally-produced foods supports the local economy, and the food tends to be fresher.

FOODS WITH HIGHEST AND LOWEST PESTICIDE RESIDUE

What fruits and vegetables are best and worst when it comes to pesticide residues? A summary of pesticides-in-food data is below. The main source of research was conducted by the Environmental Working Group (EWG), but the results have been augmented with additional information from analyses performed by Charles M. Benbrook, PhD, an agricultural specialist, and by Consumers Union.

Notice the four categories listed from worst to best. Avoid non-organic purchases from the "avoid" and "caution" columns. Even the foods listed in the "best" column were not always found to be pesticide-free, but they were consistently low in pesticide residues and are your best bet for non-organic food. An EWG simulation showed that people can lower their pesticide exposure 90% by avoiding the most contaminated fruits and vegetables.

Avoid unless Organic	Use Caution	Better—Not Perfect	Best of the Bunch
Peaches	Spinach	Applesauce	Broccoli
Apples	Grapes	Raspberries	Orange juice
Sweet bell peppers	Lettuce	Plums	Blueberry
Celery	Potatoes	Grapefruit	Papaya
Nectarines	Green beans	Tangerine	Cabbage
Strawberry	Hot peppers	Apple juice	Bananas
Cherries	Cucumber	Honeydew melon	Kiwi
Carrots	Mushroom	Tomatoes	Canned tomatoes
Pears	Cantaloupe	Sweet potatoes	Sweet peas
Frozen winter squash	Oranges	Watermelon	Asparagus
	Fresh	Cauliflower	Mango
	Winter squash		Canned pears
			Pineapple
			Corn
			Avocado
			Onion

Asparagus with Mustard Sauce

- » 2 pounds (908 g) asparagus—trimmed
- » 3 tablespoons butter
- » ¼ teaspoon salt
- » Dash of pepper
- » 1 cup (240 ml) lite sour cream
- » 2 tablespoons red wine vinegar
- » ¼ cup (60 ml) Dijon mustard
- » 1 teaspoon honey
- » ½ teaspoon onion powder

1. *Preheat oven: 450°F (230°C).*

2. *Steam the asparagus. Add the butter, salt, and pepper to the asparagus and let sit for 5 minutes under cover in original pan.*

3. *Combine ingredients for sauce (sour cream, vinegar, mustard, honey, onion powder) and cook over medium heat for 4-5 minutes.*

Serve sauce over asparagus.

 ## True Success

True success comes only when every generation continues to teach and train the next generation. This applies to healthy eating and following scriptural principles—we need to pass it on. "Train up a child in the way he should go and when he is old he will not depart from it" (Prov. 22:6).

Butternut Squash Soufflé

- » 2 cups (470 ml) butternut squash
- » 3 eggs
- » ½ cup (120 ml) sucanat with honey or honey crystals
- » 3 tablespoons butter
- » ½ teaspoon cinnamon
- » ½ teaspoon cloves
- » 1 teaspoon nutmeg
- » 1 teaspoon vanilla
- » ⅓ cup (75 ml) milk

Topping:
- » ½ cup (120 ml) honey crystals
- » 1 cup (240 ml) pecans—chopped
- » ⅓ cup (75 ml) whole wheat flour—pastry
- » ¼ cup (60 ml) melted butter

1. *Preheat oven: 325°F (163°C).*

2. *Mix all with blender and pour into greased casserole dish.*

3. *Best bites are without the extra calories of the topping but it can be added as a special treat.*

4. *Mix topping ingredients and sprinle on top before baking.*

5. *Bake 45 minutes or until soufflé is set.*

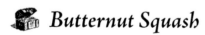 *Butternut Squash*

Butternut squash is a fall harvest vegetable that has a sweet orange flesh. It is very versatile and can be used as a side dish like oven fries, or added to soups.

Chickpea Salad

- » 1-19 ounce (532 g) can of chickpeas—drained and rinsed
- » 2 tomatoes—chopped
- » 1 cucumber—peeled and chopped
- » ½ red onion—thinly sliced
- » 1 tablespoon olive oil
- » 2 tablespoons fresh lemon juice
- » ¼ teaspoon salt

1. *Combine all ingredients and serve.*

Makes 4 servings.

Chickpeas

A favorite in the middle east, chickpeas are quickly becoming a reqested bean here in America. The most familiar serving is crushed in a dip known as hummus. Hummus makes a perfect condiment for any sandwich or salad. Chickpeas can be added to most any dish listing beans. They are also known as garbanzo beans.

Spinach Soufflé

- » 6 eggs
- » 2 cups (470 ml) cottage cheese
- » 8 ounces (224 g) extra sharp cheddar cheese
- » 1 stick butter
- » 2 packages frozen spinach
- » ¼ cup (60 ml) flour

1. *Preheat oven: 350°F (180°C).*

2. *Mix all ingredients, pour in greased casserole dish. Bake 1 hour.*

Italian Chickpeas

» 2 cans (14 ounce/392 g each) tomatoes with garlic, oregano, and basil
» 1 can chickpeas—rinsed and drained
» 1 teaspoon Italian seasoning

1. Combine tomatoes, chick peas, and seasoning in slow cooker. Cover and cook on high 3-4 hours or on low 6-8 hours.

2. Before serving, stir mixture again and season with salt and pepper to taste.

This can be a main dish or served over hot brown rice or orzo. Fresh parmesan cheese will add extra flavor on top.

Stir Fried Asparagus

» 3 tablespoons organic butter
» 1 teaspoon chicken bouillon
» ⅛ teaspoon celery seed
» ⅛ teaspoon pepper
» All purpose seasoning
» 1½ pounds (681 g) asparagus—cut and trimmed
» 1 teaspoon Bragg's Liquid Aminos

1. In a large skillet or wok, melt butter. Add bouillon, celery seed, pepper and all purpose seasoning. Mix well.

2. Add asparagus and toss to coat. Cover and cook for 2 minutes over medium heat, stirring occasionally.

3. Stir in Liquid Aminos soy sauce; serve immediately.

Chinese Green Beans

- » 1 pound (454 g) green beans
- » 1 tablespoon green onions—chopped
- » 2 garlic cloves—pressed
- » 6 thin ginger slices
- » 3 tablespoons sesame oil
- » 1 tablespoon sucanat with honey
- » ½ teaspoon salt
- » 2 tablespoons Bragg's Liquid Amino
- » ¼ cup (60 ml) water

1. *Steam green beans until crisp tender. Sauté green onions, garlic, and ginger in hot oil in a skillet for 1 minute; add sucanat, salt, and amino, and cook until this all dissolves.*

2. *Add beans and water; reduce heat to medium and stir-fry 3 minutes.*

Serve immediately.

Sesame Green Beans

- » ¾ pound (341 g) fresh green beans
- » ½ cup (120 ml) water
- » 1 tablespoon butter
- » 1 tablespoons Bragg's Liquid Aminos
- » 2 teaspoon Sesame seeds, toasted

1. *In a saucepan, bring green beans and water to a boil; reduce heat to medium.*

2. *Cover and cook for 10-15 minutes or until the beans are crisp-tender; drain. Add butter, liquid aminos, and sesame seeds; toss to coat.*

Keep the Green—Add Vitamin C

Adding a crushed vitamin C tablet to the cooking process will help keep the green beans bright green as they cook.

Grilled Summer Squash and Tomatoes

- » ¼ cup (60 ml) olive oil
- » 1 teaspoon salt
- » 4 garlic cloves—minced
- » 2 tablespoons balsamic vinegar
- » ½ teaspoon pepper
- » 1 pound (454 g) yellow squash—slices
- » 4 medium green tomatoes— cut in ¼" slices

1. *Combine first 5 ingredients in a shallow dish or in a heavy duty bag; add tomato and squash. Seal and chill 30 minutes.*

2. *Remove vegetables from marinade and reserve marinade.*

3. *Grill vegetables, covered with grill lid, over med/high heat for 10 minutes, turning occasionally. Toss with reserved marinade.*

Mixed Up Vegetables

A Savory Surprise

- » 3 cups (720 ml) cabbage— shredded—red or green
- » 1 cup (240 ml) celery—sliced
- » 1½ cup (360 ml) green pepper—chopped
- » 1½ teaspoon sea salt
- » ½ cup (120 ml) hot water
- » 2 cups (470 ml) carrots—sliced
- » 2 large onions—chopped or sliced
- » 1 tablespoon honey
- » ¼ cup (60 ml) olive oil

1. *Mix all ingredients and place in cooking saucepan. Cook until tender. About 20 minutes.*

Oven Baked Butternut Squash

» 1 whole butternut squash

1. *Preheat oven 350°*

2. *Cut one whole butternut squash into wedges. Spray cookie sheet with oil and place wedges onto pan, skin side down. Either spray wedge with oil or pour a small amount of melted butter on each wedge.*

3. *Sprinkle with The Spice Hunter Chinese Five Spice seasoning or your favorite seasonings.*

4. *Bake 30 minutes or until tender.*

Before serving, either peel off skin or eat out of skin.

Roasted Sweet Potatoes

» 4 sweet potatoes—peeled, cubed or strips
» 1 tablespoon butter or olive oil
» 1 tablespoon Spicy Ginger Stir Fry (Spice Hunter)
» 1 tablespoon All purpose Seasoning (Spice Hunter)
» ¼ teaspoon salt

1. Preheat oven: 400°F (200°C).

2. Peel uncooked sweet potatoes and dice into 1 inch squares, as you would for a potato salad. Melt butter in baking dish or pan in oven as it preheats. Place potatoes in dish, roll in melted butter. Sprinkle on seasoning.

3. Bake 45 minutes. Use metal spatula to turn potatoes every 15 minutes. Serving size approximately 6-8.

Note: This is a great vegetable to accompany almost any meal and guests will love it. You can peel and dice the potatoes ahead of time and store in a zip lock bag or container for days in the refrigerator.

Flavorful Variations

* Any of your favorite seasonings will taste good. White potatoes are good prepared this way also.
* Garlic powder and Cajun seasoning is a good blend.

Potatoes

Sweet potatoes are listed as one of the most nutritious foods we can eat. New Red Potatoes are low on the glycemic index while white potatoes are higher. This leaves the white potato left off the menu. White potatoes may cause problems for diabetics and insulin resistant individuals. Organic potatoes, in general, are nutritious with no fat. Adding these to the menu will increase satiety as long as you cut down on the toppings. Learn to enjoy the flavor of the potato instead of the toppings.

Scalloped Turnips

Surprisingly Satisfying Side Dish

- » 1 cup (240 ml) water
- » 1 cup (240 ml) milk
- » 1 teaspoon sea salt
- » 3 cups (720 ml) turnips—peeled, thinly sliced
- » 2 cups (470 ml) carrots—peeled and sliced
- » ½ cup (120 ml) onions—sliced
- » ¼ cup (60 ml) diced celery—diced
- » ⅓ cup (75 ml) green pepper—diced
- » 1 tablespoon organic butter
- » 1 cup (240 ml) cheese—cheddar, farmers or your choice
- » 5 tablespoons bread crumbs

1. *Bring water and milk to boil; add salt, turnips, carrots, onions, celery, and green peppers.*

2. *Simmer, covered about 20 minutes or until tender. Do not drain. Add butter, cheese, and breadcrumbs.*

3. *Heat, covered, until cheese is melted.*

Makes 5 servings

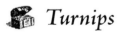 *Turnips*

The turnip is an easy to grow cruciferous vegetable loaded with nutrition. Fresh turnips are available year round with the peak season October through March. Young small turnips are sweeter and delicately flavored. Store in a cool dry place. Before using, they should be washed, trimmed and peeled. This root vegetable contributes vitamins, minerals and phytonutrients to your diet.

Stir Fry Zucchini

- » 1 tablespoon safflower oil
- » 1 pound (454 g) zucchini—cut into 1 inch pieces
- » 1 onion—cut into wedges
- » ½ teaspoon ginger—freshly grated is best
- » 1 tablespoon sesame seeds
- » 1 tablespoon Bragg's Liquid Aminos
- » 1½ teaspoon sesame oil

1. Heat safflower oil in large skillet over medium heat. Add zucchini, onion and ginger. Stir fry for about 5-6 minutes.

2. Sprinkle with sesame seeds, liquid aminos and sesame oil. Toss to mix.

Yogurtified Mashed Potatoes

- » 3 pounds (1.4 kg) russet potatoes
- » 1¼ cups (300 ml) plain yogurt
- » 1 tablespoon olive oil
- » Salt and pepper—to taste

1. Boil potatoes with skin on until done. Salt the water if desired. Drain, transfer to mixing bowl. Add yogurt and olive oil. Whip potatoes. Salt and pepper to taste.

Enticing Entrees

Fresh Market

Free range poultry, beef, & lamb

Protein

Enriching your meals with protein will benefit every cell in your body. Protein gives us these benefits:

- Protein is the single most important food we eat.
- It provides the structure for all living things.
- It is a necessary part of every living cell in the body.
- After water, protein makes up the greatest portion of body weight.
- Protein makes up muscles, ligaments, tendons, organs, glands, nails, hair, hormones, and many vital organs.
- It is needed for vitamins and minerals to be absorbed and assimilated.
- Protein provides energy directly to muscles.

Sources of protein include meat, dairy, and vegetable products. Each has about seven to eight grams of protein per one-ounce (28 g) serving. Vegetable sources of protein include legumes (such as soy), beans, and peas. Nuts (including peanuts, walnuts, pecans, and almonds) and seeds (such as pumpkin, sunflower, and flaxseed) are also excellent sources of protein.

With all these sources of protein, why should we eat meat? Meat—animal foods raised naturally—is the best source of a complete protein. This means that all nine amino acids, those essential in the diet and not formed in the body, are in the food and our body can make healthy cells. Soy is another complete protein. It requires less digestion than meat to get the nutrients available for the body to absorb. Other plants do not give the complete package. Combining beans and grains will give a meal a complete protein to build healthy cells.

ADDING BEANS IN YOUR COOKING

Beans are a great food full of nutrition and add only 2-3% fat. Beans provide protein. The proteins in beans contain smaller quantities of protein than a steak but the percentage of usable protein is over 50% (Dr. Lendon Smith Feed Your Kids Right).

For those on a budget, beans will stretch your dollars and give your family a hearty, healthy meal. Learning to cook dry beans is easy to do with a little practice. Canned beans can be used also, but the cost is more. Be sure to rinse them well to avoid the added salt and chemicals.

Using Beans in your Meal Planning:

Beans can be ground into flour and added to soups, casseroles, breads, etc. Start by substituting 2 tablespoons of your regular flour with bean flour. As you get used to the taste, increase the amount. I did this in gravy and it was very good and worked as a thickener. Add beans to your soups for a great protein pick-up and added flavor.

Common Varieties of Beans:

Black Beans—small and black, but turn a dark brown when cooked. These can be used in soups and Mediterranean dishes.

Black-Eyed Peas—small, oval shaped and creamy white with a black spot on one side. These cook more quickly than most beans and reportedly cause less gas. Use these as a main dish.

Garbanzo Beans, Chickpeas—nut-flavored and commonly pickled in vinegar and oil for salads. They can be served as a main dish, or mashed and used as a binding agent in patties or loaves.

Great Northern Beans—large white beans used in soups, salads, casseroles and baked bean dishes.

Kidney Beans—large, red colored, and kidney shaped. They are popular for chili and salads.

Lima Beans—white, broad, and flat. They make an excellent main dish and work well in soups and casseroles.

Navy Beans—include Great Northern beans—flat, small white beans, they are very versatile and can be used in any recipe calling for beans.

Pinto Beans—same species as kidney beans and used in many Mexican dishes.

Soybeans—King of all beans when it comes to protein. Ounce for ounce, the soybean contains twice as much protein as meat, four times that of eggs, and twelve times that of milk. It is the only bean that is a complete protein and is loaded with vitamins.

Dry Peas—each variety has its own distinct flavor. They can be used for flour, in soups, on salads, or can be mashed for dips.

Lentils—an old world legume with a peppery taste, are disc-shaped, and about the size of a pea. They are the easiest and fastest to cook (30 minutes) since they require no advance soaking. Like soybeans they are a complete protein including all 8 essential amino acids. They can be served raw or cooked, making soups, casseroles, patties, and croquettes.

(Information gathered from: *Country Beans* by Rita Bingham.)

COOKING BEANS

The simplest way to cook beans is to place 1 part beans, washed and cleaned, with 3 parts water in a crock pot. Cover and cook on low overnight or 9 hours until completely soft and tender. I like to prepare the beans this way and then freeze them in a Ziploc bag in 2 cup amounts. Label the bag and lay flat in the freezer for easy storage and accessibility.

The Alamo Bowl

Remember the Alamo is easy with this favorite dish.

- » 3-4 boneless, skinless chicken breast
- » 1 cup (240 ml) brown rice—cooked
- » 2 cups (470 ml) black beans—cooked
- » 2 cups (470 ml) organic corn—frozen or fresh
- » 1 can spicy stewed tomatoes
- » 1 can rotel tomatoes
- » 1 cup (240 ml) fat-free cheese—shredded
- » 1 medium avocado or guacamole—optional

1. *Preheat oven: 350°F (180°C).*

2. *Boil chicken in water until cooked thoroughly (about 20 minutes), then cut into cubes or small pieces. Place rice, beans, corn, chicken, and tomatoes in a large glass bowl, stir until mixed and top with cheese.*

3. *Bake 10 minutes in bowl or casserole dish until cheese melts. Top with avocado or a scoop of guacamole.*

Flavorful Variations

* Leftovers work well wrapped in a tortilla topped with salsa.

Quick Chicken Mexicali

» 1 whole boneless chicken or 4 chicken breasts
» 1-8 ounce (224 g) jar pizza sauce—or make your own
» 1-8 ounce (224 g) jar salsa—or make your own
» 4 cups (960 ml) brown rice—cooked

1. Cook the chicken in a crock pot with water until done. Save the chicken broth for other recipes.

2. Drain all liquid from the crock pot, cover with pizza sauce and salsa, let simmer. Serve over rice.

Makes 4 servings.

Baked Greek Spaghetti

» 1 pound (454 g) turkey—ground
» ½ onion—chopped
» 1 garlic clove—minced
» 1 package whole wheat pasta
» 2 jars favorite tomato sauce
» 1 package low fat feta cheese

1. Preheat oven: 350°F (180°C).

2. Brown turkey with onion and garlic, drain and set aside. Boil pasta with a little olive oil in water. Mix turkey, pasta and tomato sauce together and place in 2 quart (1.9 L) baking dish.

3. Sprinkle feta cheese over top and bake for 35 minutes or until bubbly.

Aloha Chicken

- » 4 boneless, skinless chicken breast halves
- » 1 tablespoon whole grain flour
- » 2 tablespoon butter
- » 2-8 ounce (224 g) cans unsweetened pineapple chunks or 2 cups (470 ml) fresh pineapple chunks
- » ¼ cup (75 ml) pineapple juice
- » 1 teaspoon organic cornstarch or Arrowroot powder
- » 1 tablespoon honey
- » 1 tablespoon Bragg's liquid aminos
- » ⅛ teaspoon pepper
- » Cooked brown rice

1. *Flatten the chicken to ¼ inch thickness. Place flour in a large resealable plastic bag, add chicken, and shake to coat. In a skillet, over medium/low heat, brown chicken in butter for 3-5 minutes on each side or until juices run clear. Remove and keep warm.*

2. *Drain pineapple, reserving ¼ cup (75 ml) juice. In a small bowl, combine cornstarch and juice until smooth. Add to skillet. Stir in honey, Bragg's liquid aminos and pepper.*

3. *Boil for 30 seconds or until thickened. Add pineapple and chicken, heat through. Serve over rice.*

Baked Parmesan Chicken

- » 2 pounds (908 g) boneless chicken breasts
- » 1 stick butter
- » 1 cup (240 ml) whole wheat bread crumbs
- » ½ cup (120 ml) parmesan cheese
- » ⅛ teaspoon salt
- » ¼ cup (60 ml) parsley—minced fresh
- » ⅛ teaspoon garlic powder
- » Paprika

1. Preheat oven: 350°F (180°C).

2. Melt butter.

3. Blend in blender: crumbs, cheese, salt, parsley, and garlic powder. Coat chicken breasts in melted butter, then coat with crumb mixture.

4. Arrange in a single layer in remaining butter in pan. Garnish with paprika and bake uncovered for 45-60 minutes.

Chicken Nuggets

Kids of all ages love these

- » 3 chicken breasts— cooked and cut into strips
- » ½ teaspoon seasoned salt
- » ⅔ cup (150 ml) wheat germ
- » ¼ teaspoon garlic powder
- » ½ cup (120 ml) water
- » 1 egg

1. Preheat oven: 400°F (200°C).

2. Mix dry ingredients. Mix water and egg. Dip chicken pieces in liquid mixture, then in dry mixture. Bake approximately 15 minutes on sprayed baking sheet for 15 minutes.

Cranberry Lemon Chicken

- » 3 pounds (1.4 kg) of chicken— cut into serving pieces
- » Salt and pepper to taste
- » 3 garlic cloves—minced
- » 2 tablespoons olive oil
- » ½ cup (120 ml) dried cranberries
- » 3 tablespoons lemon juice
- » ¼ cup (60 ml) chicken broth
- » 1 tablespoon lemon rind— finely grated
- » 1 teaspoon dried oregano
- » ½ teaspoon dried thyme

1. *Preheat oven to 400°F (200°C).*

2. *Salt and pepper the chicken pieces and rub them all over with the garlic. Place the olive oil and dried cranberries in a shallow baking dish that will hold the chicken pieces in one layer, distributing the berries evenly. Layer chicken on top.*

3. *Drizzle the lemon juice over the chicken. Pour the chicken broth around the edges. Sprinkle with lemon peel, oregano and thyme.*

4. *Bake the chicken in preheated oven for 30 minutes. Turn the chicken pieces and bake for another 30 minutes or until done.*

Makes 4 servings.

 ## Cranberries

These shiny scarlet berries are grown in big sand bogs on low trailing vines. They are extensively cultivated in Massachusetts, Wisconsin, Washington, and Oregon. Harvested September through early November, the peak market period is around Thanksgiving and Christmas. Discard any cranberries that are discolored or shriveled. Cranberries can be refrigerated, tightly wrapped for at least two months or frozen up to a year.

Broiled Salmon Fillets

Moist and Colorful

- » 4 salmon fillets—fresh (wild—not farm raised)
- » Olive oil
- » 1 green or red pepper
- » 1 medium sweet onion
- » 1 medium yellow onion
- » ¼ pineapple—fresh cut in chunks
- » ½ teaspoon dill weed
- » Salt and pepper to taste
- » 2 tablespoons lemon juice
- » 2 tablespoons honey

1. *Select fresh salmon, rinse and place on shallow baking dish/tray previously drizzled with a tablespoon of olive oil. Cut the pepper, onions, and pineapple into large slices and add to baking dish. Sprinkle the fish with dill, salt and pepper.*

2. *Drizzle fish and accompanying vegetables/fruit with lemon juice and honey. Broil until fish flakes in middle and is still moist.*

 *Salmon*

Salmon are saltwater fish that migrate to fresh waters to spawn. Wild salmon will have a more flavorful flesh and a richer supply of nutrients including omega 3. The farm raised variety are fed special diets to increase their color and nutrient content but it is still not comparable. Pacific salmon is in season spring through fall and Atlantic salmon is in season from summer to early winter.

Cheesy Broccoli Bake

» 1 pound (454 g) ground beef—organic
» 1 medium onion—chopped
» ½ cup (120ml) mushrooms—sliced, optional
» ¼ cup (60 ml) peppers, red or green—chopped, optional
» 1 garlic clove—minced
» 3 cups (720 ml) cooked brown rice
» 2 cups (470 ml) fresh or frozen broccoli
» 2 cups (470 ml) cheddar cheese—shredded
» 2 tablespoons parmesan cheese

1. *Preheat oven: 350°F (180°C).*

2. *In a skillet, cook beef, onion, mushrooms, pepper and garlic over med. heat until meat is no longer pink; drain. Stir in rice, broccoli and cheddar cheese.*

3. *Place in greased 13" x 9" baking dish. Sprinkle with parmesan cheese.*

4. *Bake uncovered for 30-40 minutes.*

Relatively quick preparation with ingredients typically on hand by everyone.

Chicken Fried Rice

A favorite by all testers!

- » 1 cup (240 ml) brown rice—cooked
- » ⅛ cup (30 ml) wild rice—cooked
- » 1 egg
- » 1 tablespoon olive oil
- » 3 garlic cloves—minced
- » 3 carrots—diced
- » 2 stalks celery—diced
- » 1 small sweet onion—diced
- » ⅔ cup (150 ml) peas—frozen
- » ½ cup (120 ml) bean sprouts
- » 1 chicken breast—cooked and diced
- » 1 tablespoon Bragg's Liquid Amino

1. *Steam rice together. Set aside. Coat a large skillet with olive oil and cook one egg, breaking the yoke to flatten the egg. Chop the cooked egg and set aside.*

2. *Sauté in the skillet: garlic, carrots, celery, onion, and peas. May add bean sprouts.*

3. *When all is tender add to the pan: chicken, egg, and rice. Add Bragg's Liquid Amino and enjoy.*

Country Sausage

- » 2 pounds (908 g) ground turkey, venison, or organic beef
- » ½ tablespoon sea salt
- » ½ tablespoon ground black pepper
- » 2½ tablespoons rubbed sage
- » 1 tablespoon Italian seasoning
- » ½ tablespoon crushed red pepper

1. *Mix together and chill for 8 hours. Make patties to broil in oven stir fry or use in favorite recipe.*

Chicken Rotel

- » 1-8 oz. package large noodles
- » 5 chicken breasts—cooked and diced
- » 1 large green pepper—chopped or ⅓ cup (80 ml) frozen
- » 1 cup (240 ml) sharp cheddar cheese—shredded
- » 1 teaspoon chili powder
- » Salt and pepper to taste
- » 1 can mushroom soup (West Brae, Amy's)
- » 1 can Rotel tomatoes

1. *Preheat oven: 375°F (190°C).*

2. *Prepare noodles and drain. Layer noodles on lightly greased 9" x 13" dish.*

3. *Mix remaining ingredients except chicken and cheese to make a sauce. Layer chicken, sauce, and top with cheese.*

4. *Bake for 30 minutes.*

Flavorful Variations

* A more healthful alternative is to make a white sauce, which is easier than it looks and cheaper than the purchased soup!

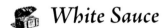 ## White Sauce

1-4 oz can sliced mushrooms
¾ cup (180 ml) flour
Drain mushrooms. Save the liquid. Put liquid in cup and add milk to equal 1½ cups (360 ml) . Mix flour with milk mixture. Heat on medium, stir frequently until thickened.

Dijon Chicken Grill

- » 4 chicken breasts
- » ¼ cup (60 ml) parsley—fresh
- » 1 teaspoon black pepper
- » 1 tablespoon olive oil
- » ¼ cup (60 ml) Dijon mustard
- » 1 teaspoon rosemary
- » 1 garlic clove
- » 2 teaspoons lemon juice

1. Mix ingredients; coat chicken. Cook 7 minutes each side on hot grill.

Savory Pot Roast

- » 1 chuck roast
- » ½ cup (120 ml) Bragg's Liquid Amino
- » 6 bay leaves
- » 1 large onion—sliced
- » 6 carrots—sliced 4" pieces
- » Fresh mushrooms
- » 3 potatoes—cut into large cubes
- » 2 tablespoons seasoned salt (Bragg's)

1. Brown roast. Place all ingredients in crock-pot in order given except carrots and mushrooms. Cook on low for 4 hours and then add carrots and mushrooms, placing them under the roast as you flip it. Flip the roast every hour or so.

2. Cook on low another 4 hours. After about 8 hours the meat should tear apart easily. Allow to sit in gravy before serving.

Turkey/Beef Hamburgers

Really moist and tasty!

- » 1 pound (454 g) ground organic sirloin or chuck beef
- » 1 pound (454 g) ground turkey
- » ½ cup (120 ml) onion—minced
- » 2 teaspoons Mrs. Dash grilling blends (steak)
- » ¼ teaspoon celery salt
- » ½ cup (120 ml) Bragg's Liquid Amino
- » ¼ cup (60 ml) organic barbecue sauce

1. Mix ingredients.

2. Form into hamburger patties and grill.

Honey Mustard Baked Chicken

- » 4 boneless skinless chicken breasts
- » ⅓ cup (75 ml) Italian dressing
- » 3 garlic cloves—minced
- » 2 teaspoons dry mustard
- » 2 tablespoons honey
- » 1 teaspoon salt

1. Preheat oven: 400°F (200°C)

2. Place chicken in a glass casserole dish that has a cover. Combine Italian dressing, garlic, mustard, honey, and salt. Pour over chicken.

3. Cover casserole dish and bake for one hour or until chicken is cooked through.

Honey Glazed Chicken

Our Family's Most Requested Meal

- » 2 pounds (908 g) chicken tenders or strips
- » 1 cup (240 ml) whole wheat flour
- » 2 teaspoons salt
- » ¼ teaspoon pepper
- » 2 teaspoons paprika
- » 3 tablespoons butter— melted
- » ¼ cup (60 ml) honey
- » ¼ cup (60 ml) butter—melted
- » ¼ cup (60 ml) lemon juice

1. *Preheat oven: 350°F (180°C).*

2. *Combine flour, salt, pepper, and paprika. Dip chicken in mix. Roll chicken in 3 tablespoons of melted butter. Lay in single layer in Pyrex dish. Bake uncovered for 30 minutes.*

3. *Combine honey, ¼ cup (60 ml) butter, and lemon juice. Turn chicken.*

4. *Pour honey sauce over chicken and bake 30 more minutes or until tender. Baste occasionally.*

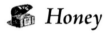 *Honey*

The best choice for honey is to buy pure, raw, unheated honey. When you find this quality of honey you will have a treasure of over a hundred nutrients that are beneficial to your body.

Makeover Lasagna

- » 9 lasagna noodles
- » 1 pound (454 g) ground beef or turkey
- » 1 jar spaghetti sauce
- » 1 pound (454 g) tofu—silken
- » 1 cup (240 ml) cottage cheese
- » ¾ cup (180 ml) parmesan cheese
- » 1 egg
- » 1 pound (454 g) mozzarella cheese—shredded

1. Preheat oven: 350°F (180°C).

2. Cook noodles according to package directions. Drain and set aside.

3. Brown meat and drain. Stir in spaghetti sauce.

4. Combine tofu, cottage cheese, parmesan cheese and egg.

5. In a 9" x 13" pan spoon a little spaghetti sauce. Layer noodles, sauce, cheese mixture, and mozzarella-twice. Finish with noodles, sauce and mozzarella.

6. Bake for about 45 minutes or until bubbly and hot throughout the dish.

Marinated Chicken

- » 5 chicken breasts—de-boned
- » Italian or Tuscany dressing

1. Marinate chicken breasts with enough dressing to cover overnight or all day if possible.

2. Grill on outdoor grill for approximately 20 minutes. Turn during cooking, continue to brush on marinade. Really moist!

Nacho Casserole

A Hearty, One-dish Fiesta!

- » 1 pound (454 g) ground chuck, turkey or venison
- » 1 medium onion—chopped
- » 1½ cups (360 ml) salsa—chunky style
- » 3 cups (720 ml) refried beans *
- » 8 ounces (224 g) cheddar cheese—shredded, divided
- » ½ cup (120 ml) water
- » 1 teaspoon chili powder
- » 1-15 ounce (420 g) bag organic blue tortilla chips—coarsely crushed
- » 2 tomatoes—chopped
- » 3 green onions—thinly sliced
- » 1-4 ounce (112 g) can sliced ripe olives—drained
- » Sour cream or yo-cheese

* recipe in this book.

1. Preheat oven: 350°F (180°C).

2. In a large skillet over medium-high heat, brown meat with onion. Drain off excess drippings. Stir in salsa, beans, 1 cup (240 ml) of cheese, water and chili powder.

3. Place half of the tortilla chips in lightly sprayed 9" x 13" dish. Cover with meat mixture.

4. Bake for 25 minutes or until heated throughout. Top with remaining tortilla chips and cheese. Bake an additional 5-7 minutes. Let stand 5 minutes before cutting into squares to serve.

5. Garnish each serving with tomatoes, green onions, olives and sour cream.

Makes 8 servings.

Patti's French Beef

A Crowd Pleaser

- » 1 package egg noodles—wide, organic
- » 1-8 ounce (224 g) package of Neufchatel cream cheese
- » 1 cup (240 ml) sour cream or yogurt—drained
- » 1 pound (454 g) organic ground beef
- » 1-16 ounce (448 g) jar spaghetti sauce—organic
- » mozzarella and cheddar cheese—shredded

1. *Preheat oven: 350°F (180°C).*

2. *Cook egg noodles according to package directions, drain, and add cream cheese to hot noodles. Stir to melt cream cheese and add sour cream. Put hot mixture in bottom of large, oiled casserole dish.*

3. *Brown ground beef, drain, and add spaghetti sauce. Cook down some. Pour over noodle mixture.*

4. *Top with shredded cheese and bake for 30 minutes or until heated through and cheese is melted.*

 *Neufchatel*

Cream cheese labeled as "Neufchatel" is 33% lower in fat than regular cream cheese. "Neufchatel" has a softer texture and a very high moisture content.

Make Your Own Spaghetti Sauce

- » 2 tablespoon olive oil
- » 1 onion—chopped
- » ½ cup (120 ml) sweet pepper—chopped
- » 1-8 ounce (224 g) can tomato sauce + 1 can water
- » 4 cups (960 ml) canned tomatoes
- » 1 teaspoon salt
- » Black pepper to taste
- » 3 tablespoon Italian seasoning
- » 1 tablespoon honey
- » 2 or 3 bay leaves
- » 2 garlic cloves—minced
- » 1 can sliced mushrooms and juice—optional

1. *Sauté onion and pepper in oil about 5 minutes. Add tomato sauce and tomatoes, salt, pepper, Italian seasoning, honey, bay leaves, garlic, mushrooms and juice.*

2. *Simmer at least 1 hour, or longer if possible. It is better to simmer very slowly until most of the juice cooks out.*

This sauce can be made ahead of time and frozen until ready to use, or freeze in smaller portions for serving fewer people.

Southwestern Pizza

» pizza crust—your favorite recipe
» ½ cup (120 ml) salsa
» 2 cups (470 ml) black beans—mashed
» 3 grilled chicken breasts—chopped
» ½ cup (120 ml) green pepper—diced
» ½ cup (120 ml) red pepper—diced
» 1 onion—chopped
» 2 cups (470 ml) Monterey jack cheese

1. *Preheat oven: 400°F (200°C).*

2. *Roll out dough on lightly-sprayed pizza pan or cookie sheet after 2nd kneading. Let rise about 10 minutes.*

3. *Combine salsa and black beans and spread evenly over crust.*

4. *Top with remaining ingredients, adding cheese last.*

5. *Bake approximately 15-20 minutes. Be careful not to overcook.*

Make Your Own Salsa

- » 1 can (14 ounces/392 g) organic diced tomatoes—well drained
- » ¼ cup (60 ml) chopped onion
- » 2 tablespoons chopped fresh cilantro
- » ¼ teaspoon sea salt
- » 1 garlic clove—minced
- » 1 small fresh jalapeno chili—seeded, finely chopped

1. Blend all ingredients together. Store in refrigerator.

Make Your Own Pizza Sauce

5-Star Delight

- » 2 garlic cloves, minced
- » ½ teaspoon salt
- » 1 can (6 ounces/168 g) tomato paste
- » 1 can (8 ounces/224 g) tomato sauce
- » ½ teaspoon sucanat or honey crystals
- » ⅛ teaspoon pepper
- » ½ teaspoon oregano
- » 1 tablespoon olive oil
- » Dash red pepper, optional

1. Combine all ingredients.

Makes about 1½ cups, enough for 2 pizzas.

Pizza Pie

- » 1 baked whole wheat pie crust—bake empty shell at 450° for 8 minutes
- » 1 pound (454 g) ground turkey sausage
- » 1 small onion—chopped
- » 4 eggs
- » 1 cup (240 ml) cheddar cheese—shredded
- » ½ cup (120 ml) soy milk
- » ½ teaspoon dried oregano
- » ⅛ teaspoon pepper
- » 1-8 ounce (224 g) jar pizza sauce—or make your own with better ingredients
- » 2 cups (470 ml) farmers cheese—grated, substitute cheddar if needed

1. Preheat oven: 350°F (180°C).

2. In large skillet brown the turkey sausage with the onion until no longer pink; drain. In a bowl beat eggs, stir in cheese, milk, oregano and pepper. Add to sausage. Pour into baked crust. Bake for 30-35 minutes or until a knife inserted comes out clean. Top with sauce and cheese.

3. Bake 5-8 minutes longer, or until cheese is melted. Let stand for 10 minutes before cutting.

Makes 6 servings.

Poulet Yassa

I acquired this recipe while on mission in Senegal, Africa. It became a favorite. The magic cubes are bouillon cubes that can be substituted with your homemade chicken broth.

» 1-2 chickens—cut up
» Oil to brown chicken
» 6-8 onions—sliced
» 5-6 carrots—thinly sliced
» 2-3 tomatoes—quartered
» 4 large Magic cubes
» ½ cup (120 ml) lemon juice—freshly squeezed
» dash of vinegar
» ⅓ cup (75 ml) oil
» 1 bay leaf
» 10-12 peppercorns
» 1 red hot pepper—optional
» 2-3 tablespoons Dijon mustard
» ½ cup (120 ml) green olives—chopped
» brown rice—cooked

1. Brown chicken in hot oil and drain.

2. In large bowl, combine chicken, onions, carrots, tomatoes, bouillon cubes, lemon juice, vinegar, and oil. Let marinate for 1 hour minimum.

3. Place in large cooking pot. Add bay leaf, peppercorns, and hot pepper. Cook over very low heat for 2-3 hours. Stir in Dijon mustard and olives.

4. Cook until hot. Serve over hot rice.

Quinoa Stir Fry

Serves a Hungry Family of Four

- » 2 cups (470 ml) quinoa—cooked in 4 cups of water
- » 3 tablespoons sesame oil
- » 2 stalks broccoli—chopped
- » 1 cup (240 ml) snow peas
- » 3 green onions—chopped
- » 3 garlic cloves—chopped
- » 1 tablespoon ginger—grated
- » 1 whole chicken—cut up and grilled
- » 1 tablespoon maple syrup
- » Bragg's Liquid Amino to taste

1. *To cook quinoa: add quinoa grains to boiling water, reduce heat and let simmer 15 minutes until water is absorbed.*

2. *Stir fry vegetables and ginger and garlic in 2-3 tablespoons sesame oil until tender.*

3. *Add maple syrup after vegetables are done.*

4. *Add chicken, quinoa and stir. If desired, add Bragg's Liquid Amino to taste.*

 ## Quinoa

Quinoa (keen-wa) is a grain grown in South America. It can be used as an alternative to brown rice, wild rice, bulgur, or millet in any recipe or menu. Quinoa is comparatively pricey; yet when served as a meatless main dish with other ingredients added, it is still less costly than many typical American meat dishes. Quinoa has a unique and delightfully light texture. It is high in protein, containing all eight essential amino acids. For a whole grain, it has very high fiber content. It is versatile as a main dish, side dish, or in salads and desserts. Try all the quinoa recipes in this book for a delight. They are very tasteful—especially the pilaf.

Parmesan Pesto Chicken

A versatile dish, bursting with flavor. Serve it hot for a dinner party or cold at your next cookout.

- » 12 ounce (336 g) brown rice pasta
- » 1 pound (454 g) boneless skinless chicken breast—cut into ½ inch slices
- » salt and freshly ground pepper
- » 1 tablespoon olive oil
- » 2 garlic cloves—minced
- » ¼ cup (60 ml) green onions—thinly sliced
- » ½ cup (120 ml) pecans—chopped
- » ½ cup (120 ml) chicken broth
- » ½ cup (120 ml) basil pesto
- » 1 tablespoon fresh cilantro—chopped
- » ½ cup (120 ml) Parmesan cheese
- » 1 pinch crushed red pepper

1. Cook pasta according to package directions, drain and set aside.

2. Season chicken with salt and pepper and sauté in olive oil on medium high heat until cooked through. Add garlic, green onions and pecans and cook one minute.

3. Stir in pasta, chicken broth, and pesto, cooking until pasta is hot and completely coated with pesto.

4. Remove from heat and stir in cilantro, Parmesan cheese, and crushed red pepper. Serve with extra Parmesan cheese on the side.

Salsa Couscous Chicken

- » 3 cups couscous or brown rice—cooked
- » ¼ cup (60 ml) almonds—chopped
- » 2 garlic cloves—minced
- » 8 chicken thighs
- » 1 cup (240 ml) salsa—chunky style
- » ¼ cup (60 ml) water
- » 2 tablespoons dried currants
- » 1 tablespoon honey
- » ½ teaspoon cumin
- » ½ teaspoon cinnamon
- » 1 tablespoon olive oil

1. Heat oil in a large skillet over medium high heat until hot. Add almonds and cook 1-2 minutes or until golden brown. Remove almonds from skillet with slotted spoon and set aside. Add garlic to skillet. Cook and stir for 30 seconds.

2. Add chicken and cook 4-5 minutes or until browned, turning once. In a medium bowl, combine salsa, water, currants, honey, cumin, and cinnamon. Mix well.

3. Add to chicken and mix well. Reduce heat to medium, cover and cook for 20 minutes or until chicken is fork tender and juices run clear. Stir in almonds. Serve with couscous or brown rice.

Makes 6 servings.

Salsa Mini Meatloaves

- » 1 pound (454 g) ground turkey, organic beef, or venison
- » ½ cup (120 ml) finely chopped onions
- » 1 egg
- » ½ cup (120 ml) whole wheat bread crumbs
- » 1½ cups (360 ml) shredded cheese, your choice
- » 1 cup (240 ml) salsa

1. Preheat oven to 400°F (200°C).

2. Mix ground meat, onions, egg, bread crumbs, and ½ cup each of cheese and salsa. Press evenly into 12 muffin cups lightly oiled. Use back of spoon to make indentation in center of each. Place muffin pan on baking sheet.

3. Bake 20-25 minutes or until meatloaves are done. Top with remaining salsa and cheese and bake 3 minutes, or until cheese it melted.

The Best Ever Sloppy Joes

Never go back to canned again!

- » 1 pound (454 g) ground turkey
- » 1- 8 ounce (224 g) can no-salt added, organic tomato sauce
- » ½ cup (120 ml) organic ketchup
- » 1½ tablespoons Worcestershire sauce
- » 1 teaspoon yellow mustard
- » ½ teaspoon dry mustard
- » 1 teaspoon molasses
- » 1 garlic clove—minced
- » pinch ground cloves
- » hot pepper sauce—to taste
- » ½ small onion—finely chopped
- » 6 whole wheat hamburger buns

1. *In large skillet brown turkey. In a sauce pan over low heat, combine sauce ingredients. Mix well and simmer. Add turkey to sauce.*

2. *Heat for 5 minutes (make sure all ingredients have been added). Spoon ½ cup (120 ml) turkey mixture over bun.*

Spelt Chapatti

Chapatti is a favorite bread throughout India. The ingredients for this chapatti recipe are simple: flour, water, salt and oil, but it takes practice to make them just right. Traditionally, chapatti is made in a Tawa, which is a slightly concave, round griddle.

- » ½ cup (120 ml) water
- » 1 tablespoon oil
- » ½ teaspoon salt
- » 2 cups (470 ml) spelt flour

1. Preheat oven: 375°F (190°C).

2. Combine water, oil and salt in a large mixing bowl.

3. Add the flour gradually, stirring until the mixture is too thick to stir. Continue to add flour, working it in with your hands until a soft dough forms. Knead until smooth. This process can be done in a food processor. Keep dough moist for chewy bread or drier for crispy chips. Let dough rest, covered, for 10-20 minutes. Form the dough into 2" balls. Flatten into 5" circles. Place on oiled baking sheet and bake for 2-3 minutes. Turn and bake an additional 2-3 minutes. Can also be cooked on oiled griddle or tortilla maker.

Top with desired ingredients: cheese, onions, tomatoes, peppers, meat, olives, beans, etc.

Spinach-Zucchini Casserole

Surprisingly, husbands and kids like this dish!

- » 3 medium zucchini—grated, about 2 pounds (908 g)
- » ½ teaspoon salt
- » 4 tablespoons butter
- » 1 large onion—peeled, chopped
- » 1-10 ounce (280 g) frozen chopped spinach—thawed and squeezed dry
- » ½ teaspoon ground thyme
- » freshly ground pepper
- » 1 cup (240 ml) Swiss cheese or Farmers cheese—grated
- » 1 cup (240 ml) yogurt (slightly drained) or sour cream
- » ½ cup (120 ml) whole wheat dry bread crumbs
- » 2 tablespoons Parmesan cheese

1. Preheat oven: 350°F (180°C).

2. Place grated zucchini in colander, sprinkle with salt, and let stand about 45 minutes.

3. Melt 3 tablespoons butter in a large skillet. Add onion, cook about 4 minutes, or until onion is clear.

4. Place zucchini between several layers of paper towels and squeeze out as much liquid as possible. Add drained zucchini to skillet and cook for 5 minutes, stirring constantly. Add spinach, thyme and pepper to skillet. Stir well.

5. Cook for 4 minutes. Remove skillet from heat. Stir in Swiss or Farmers cheese until melted. Stir in yogurt.

6. Spoon mixture into a 1½ quart (1.4 L) baking dish that has been sprayed with olive oil. Sprinkle bread crumbs and parmesan cheese on top. Dot with remaining 1 tablespoon butter.

7. Bake, uncovered for 25-30 minutes.

Stromboli

Feed a crowd of hungry sports fans, or a hungry family for a casual supper, with this rolled, baked sandwich. Any combination of meats, cheeses and vegetables can vary the taste of this dish, so take our suggestions with a grain of salt. One hint however, the more vegetables you use, the more liquid they'll release, so too many vegetables can make a somewhat soggy Stromboli. Use as many different fillings as you like, but it's important to not layer them too thickly, as this will make it difficult to roll the Stromboli.

Another great thing about this sandwich is that it's good cold, making it not only perfect for football parties but for picnics as well.

Dough:
- » 1¼ cups (300 ml) warm water (105°-115°F/40-46°C)
- » 1 tablespoon yeast
- » 1 teaspoon sucanat, either variety
- » 2 tablespoons olive oil
- » 2 teaspoons salt
- » 3½ to 4 cups (840-960 ml) whole wheat flour—hard white

1. Combine ¼ cup (60 ml) warm water, yeast and sucanat in a large bowl and stir to dissolve. Let stand until foamy, about 5 minutes. Stir in remaining warm water, olive oil, and salt. Gradually add 1½ to 2 cups (360-470 ml) flour, mixing until smooth. Gradually add enough remaining flour until you have a smooth dough that comes away from the bowl. Turn dough out onto a lightly floured surface and knead 10 minutes, working in more flour as needed. Shape into a ball, place in a greased bowl and cover with a clean kitchen towel. Let dough rise until doubled, about 1 hour.

2. Preheat oven to 375°F (190°C).

3. Grease a large baking sheet. (If you have a pizza or bread stone in your oven you can forego the baking sheet and bake the Stromboli directly on the stone. A French loaf pan works well for this recipe also.)

Punch dough down and cut in half. On a lightly floured surface, roll each dough half into a rectangle about 10 x 8". Arrange fillings over dough, finishing with a sprinkling of Parmesan cheese. Roll the dough much like you would if you were making a jelly roll. Pinch the edges of the seam and tuck the ends under. Bake for 30 minutes.

Veggie Stromboli

- » ½ cup (120 ml) olive oil
- » 3 garlic cloves—minced
- » 3 yellow onions—chopped
- » 4 medium tomatoes—diced
- » 4 cups spinach
- » 1 teaspoon dried basil
- » cracked black pepper
- » 1 teaspoon oregano
- » ½ teaspoon salt
- » 2 cups (470 ml) cheese
- » bread dough from your favorite recipe

1. *Cook all ingredients except bread dough for approximately 30-40 minutes over medium heat until very tender. Sprinkle with any kind of cheese.*

2. *Add about two cups of mixture and follow directions listed above for Stromboli.*

Philly Cheese Stromboli

- » ½ cup (120 ml) yo-cheese or low fat mayonnaise
- » 2½ teaspoons Italian seasoning
- » ½ teaspoon pepper
- » 1 large onion—thinly sliced
- » 2 medium green peppers—sliced thinly
- » 1 stalk celery—diced
- » 1 tablespoon olive oil
- » 1 pound (454 g) roast beef—sliced thinly
- » 1½ cups provolone cheese—slices

Dough:
- » 1¼ cups (300 ml) warm water (105°-115°F/40-46°C)
- » 1 tablespoon yeast
- » 1 teaspoon sucanat, either variety
- » 2 tablespoons olive oil
- » 2 teaspoons salt
- » 3½ to 4 cups (840-960 ml) whole wheat flour—hard white

1. *Combine mayonnaise, seasoning, and pepper. Set aside. Cook onion, green pepper strips and celery in olive oil in a large skillet over medium heat until tender, stirring often.*

2. *Roll dough in rectangle. Arrange half of roast beef on dough and spread half mayonnaise mixture on top. Layer half of vegetable mixture over cheese. Top with layer of provolone cheese slices. Repeat layers.*

Dessert Stromboli

Roll out dough as above. Drizzle with honey. Sprinkle with cinnamon. Cover with dried coconut, chopped nuts, and raisins. Roll and bake.

Salmon Cakes

- » 12-16 ounces (454 gms.) fresh salmon (wild caught)
- » 1 teaspoon Old Bay seasoning
- » 3 tablespoon onion—chopped
- » 3 tablespoon celery—chopped
- » 3 tablespoon green pepper—chopped (optional)
- » 2-3 eggs(depending on size)
- » 1-1½ cups (240 ml—360 ml) bread crumbs
- » ½ teaspoon salt
- » dash of pepper
- » olive oil

1. *Preheat oven: 350°F (180°C).*

2. *Place fresh salmon in oil/greased shallow pan. Sprinkle Old Bay seasoning on top of salmon. Bake in oven for 15-20 minutes or until salmon flakes easily with a fork.*

3. *Remove salmon without skin and crumble in bowl.*

4. *Add onion, celery, green pepper, eggs, bread crumbs, salt and pepper. Mix together. Make into patties, flour both sides and cook in fry pan (bottom covered with olive oil). Brown both sides of patties on medium heat, remove from pan and serve hot.*

Makes 6-8 patties.

≈ Flavorful Variations

* Canned wild salmon is an option. Drain and remove skin and bones and crumble to make patties.

Stuffed Peppers

- » 1 pound (454 g) ground sirloin
- » ½ cup (120 ml) celery—finely chopped
- » ½ cup (120 ml) onions—chopped
- » ½ teaspoon salt
- » ½ teaspoon ginger
- » 3 tablespoons cornstarch, non GMO (will state this on label)
- » 3 tablespoons olive oil
- » 4 tablespoons Bragg's Liquid Amino
- » 4 peppers
- » 1½ cups (360 ml) beef broth
- » 4 cups (960 ml) brown rice—cooked

1. *In a medium bowl mix beef, celery, onions, salt, ginger, 1 tablespoon of cornstarch, 1 tablespoon of olive oil, and 1 tablespoon of Bragg's. Stuff into prepared peppers (cut peppers in half and remove seeds and stems).*

2. *In a large skillet add olive oil, arrange peppers stuffed side up. Add broth and simmer, covered for 35 minutes.*

3. *Place peppers on warm platter of rice. Pour off pan liquid, reserving 1 cup (240 ml). Return reserved liquid to skillet.*

4. *In a cup, dissolve 2 tablespoons of cornstarch, in 3 tablespoons of Bragg's. Gradually add to skillet and cook over medium heat, stirring until thickened. Pour over peppers and rice.*

Makes 5 servings.

Mexican Bean Bake

» ½ cup (120 ml) pinto bean flour
» 2 cups (470 ml) vegetable stock
» ½ cup (120 ml) green chili salsa
» ½ large onion—grated
» 2 cups (470 ml) brown rice—cooked
» 6 corn tortillas—cut in fourths
» 1½ cups jack cheese—grated, optional

1. *Preheat oven: 350°F (180°C).*

2. *Whisk bean flour into vegetable stock, bring to a boil. Add salsa and onions, and then bring back to a boil. Cook for 3 minutes over medium heat. In a 1 quart (.95 L) baking dish layer rice, ½ tortillas and ½ salsa mixture.*

3. *Top with tortillas, salsa mixture, and cheese. Bake until cheese bubbles, about 10-15 minutes. Cover if you omit the cheese.*

Makes 4-6 servings.

 *Tortilla*

Tortillas add a fun flair to meals and come in a variety of flavors. When choosing a corn or white flour tortilla, look for organic to avoid the GMO corn or wheat. Recipes for making your own can be found on the Designed Healthy Living web site, titled *It's a Wrap.*

Tortilla Bean Casserole

- » 2 cups (470 ml) onions—chopped
- » 1½ cups (360 ml) green pepper—chopped
- » 1-14 ounce (392 g) canned tomatoes
- » 1 cup (240 ml) picante sauce
- » 2 garlic cloves
- » 2 teaspoons cumin
- » 2-15 ounce (420 g) cans black beans—rinsed
- » 12 tortillas
- » 3 cups (720 ml) Monterey jack cheese—shredded or your favorite cheese
- » 2 medium tomatoes—chopped
- » 2 cups (470 ml) lettuce—shredded
- » green onion—sliced
- » black olives—sliced
- » ½ cup (120 ml) sour cream

1. *Preheat oven: 350°F (180°C).*

2. *In a medium saucepan combine onion, green pepper, canned tomatoes in juices, picante sauce, garlic, and cumin. Bring to a boil. Reduce heat and simmer uncovered for 10 minutes. Stir in drained beans.*

3. *In 13" x 9" baking dish spread $^1/_3$ of mixture over the bottom. Top with tortillas, overlapping a bit as needed. Sprinkle 1 cup (240 ml) of cheese on tortillas. Add $^1/_3$ more of mixture and continue layers until everything is gone.*

4. *Cover and bake for 30 minutes until bubbly. Remove from oven, sprinkle with 1 cup (240 ml) of cheese for topping; let stand until cheese melts.*

5. *Top with tomatoes, lettuce, green onions, and black olives. Serve sour cream on side.*

Turkey Cuban Style

- » 1 turkey breast
- » 2 cups (470 ml) orange juice or lime juice
- » ½ cup (120 ml) Worcestershire sauce
- » seasoning salt
- » 8 carrots, sliced
- » ½ cup (120 ml) water
- » ¼ cup (60 ml) spicy mustard

1. *Preheat oven: 350°F (180°C).*

2. *Place turkey breast in large baking dish with enough room to add carrots later. Pour liquid ingredients over turkey; rub mustard and seasoning salt all over. Marinate for 24 hours for better flavor.*

3. *Place in oven, uncovered, with an inserted meat thermometer.*

4. *Cook on set temperature until meat thermometer indicates done for poultry.*

5. *Baste with gravy marinade every 30-40 minutes. Add carrots after 1 hour. If needed, cover the top of turkey with a little tin foil toward the end of the second hour.*

Vegetable Lasagna

» 16 ounce (448 g) box lasagna—cooked, drained
» 3 pounds (1.4 kg) ricotta cheese
» 8 ounce (224 g) yo-cheese
» 1 cup (240 ml) onion—minced
» 2 teaspoons dried basil
» 1 garlic clove—fresh, minced
» 1 cup (240 ml) broccoli—chopped
» 1 cup (240 ml) zucchini—chopped
» 1 cup (240 ml) mushrooms—diced
» 1 cup (240 ml) spinach leaves—chopped
» 4 cups (960 ml) mozzarella—shredded
» 1 cup (240 ml) Parmesan cheese

1. Preheat oven: 375°F (190°C).

2. Mix together ricotta cheese, yo cheese, onion, basil and garlic. Stir in vegetables.

3. In a 9" x 13" pan, layer noodles, vegetable mixture, mozzarella and Parmesan cheese. Continue layers, ending with cheeses.

4. Bake for 50 minutes. Allow to cool for 10 minutes.

Flavorful Variations

* Vegetables can vary with season. Other vegetables to use in recipe include but are not limited to: yellow squash, carrots, cauliflower, and peas.

Savory Soups

& Stews

Savory Soups and Stews

Soups and stews are a satisfying and great way to incorporate whole foods into the diet of your family. Beans, vegetables, and grains can all be added to any soup to make it more wholesome. Experiment and see what new recipes you may come up with that your family enjoys.

SOUP BROTH

Make your own broth for an economical healthy alternative to store purchases. Store-bought broth may contain MSG and too much salt. Here are some tips for making your own:

In 4 quarts (3.8 L) of water place 4-6 pounds (1.8-2.7 kg) of meat pieces and bones. Use turkey, chicken, beef, or venison. Bring this to a boil and then add carrots, onions, celery leaves, 3 tablespoons apple cider vinegar, bay leaf, salt, parsley, and 1 teaspoon of thyme. Cook on low for 8-10 hours in a crock pot. Strain. Refrigerate. When the fat has risen to the top, skim it off and then freeze in desired proportions.

Soup Broth—Your Key to Getting Calcium

Many Asians prepare a stock from bones that helps account for their adequate calcium intake without the use of milk. They soak the cracked bones from chicken, turkey, and fish in vinegar and then slowly boil the bones until they become soft. The bones release calcium into the acidic broth, and most of the vinegar boils off. Cooks then use the stock, which contains more than 100 milligrams of calcium per tablespoon, in the place of water to prepare soups, vegetables, and rice.

Black Bean Soup

Quick and Easy

- » 1 cup (240 ml) fresh tomato salsa
- » 2-15 ounce cans (420 g) black beans—drained, rinsed
- » 2 cups (470 ml) chicken broth (free range)
- » Plain non fat yogurt
- » Chives for topping

1. *Heat the salsa in a large saucepan over medium heat, stirring frequently, for about 5 minutes.*

2. *Stir in the beans and broth, heat to boiling. Reduce heat to low. Cover and simmer for 15 minutes. Cool slightly. Spoon half the soup into a food processor or blender and puree. Return the pureed soup to the saucepan and heat throughout. Serve with a dollop of plain yogurt and chopped chives.*

Makes 4 servings.

Southwestern Chicken Soup

Pleasing to the appetite while easy on budget and waistline.

- » 2 teaspoons olive oil
- » 1¼ pounds (568 g) boneless, skinless chicken—cubed
- » 2-14.5 ounce (406 g) cans low sodium organic chicken broth
- » 16 ounces (448 g) organic corn—frozen
- » 1-14 ounce (392 g) can diced tomatoes
- » 1 medium onion—chopped
- » 1 medium green pepper—chopped
- » 1 medium sweet red pepper—chopped
- » 1-4 ounce (112 g) can chopped green chili
- » 1½ teaspoons seasoned salt
- » 1 teaspoon ground cumin
- » 2 garlic cloves—minced

1. Brown chicken in large skillet with olive oil over medium heat. Transfer to a 5 quart (4.75 L) slow cooker and add remaining ingredients. Cover and cook on low for 7-8 hours.

2. Soup can be served as a main dish along with a fresh green salad, homemade dressing, and a whole grain roll.

Carol's Brown Stew

Home-Cooked Goodness

- » 2 pounds (908 g) of lean beef—cut into cubes
- » 2 tablespoons olive oil
- » 6 cups (1.5 L) water—boiling—add more if needed
- » 2 tablespoons whole wheat flour
- » 1 teaspoon lemon juice
- » 1 teaspoon Worcestershire sauce
- » 1 garlic clove—minced
- » 1 medium onion—sliced
- » 2 bay leaves
- » 1 tablespoon salt
- » 1 teaspoon pepper
- » ½ teaspoon paprika
- » dash allspice or cloves
- » 1 tablespoon honey
- » 6 carrots—quartered
- » 4 small onions, quartered or 2 medium onions sliced
- » 2 potatoes—cubed

1. *Thoroughly brown meat on all sides in oil. Add water, flour, lemon juice, Worcestershire sauce, garlic, onion, bay leaves, and seasoning.*

2. *Simmer 2 hours. Stir occasionally to keep from sticking. Add carrots, onions, and potatoes. Cook until done.*

Makes 6-8 servings.

Butternut Squash Soup

Flavorful, Low Fat, High in Fiber

- » 2 tablespoon extra virgin olive oil, or butter
- » 1 medium onion, diced
- » 3 garlic cloves, minced
- » 2 teaspoons ground cumin
- » 2 pounds (908 g) butternut squash, peeled and diced
- » 2 large sweet potatoes, peeled and cubed
- » 1 large rutabaga, peeled and cubed
- » 1 turnip, peeled and cubed
- » 4 cups (960 ml) vegetable stock or chicken broth
- » 2 tablespoons maple syrup
- » 1½ teaspoon salt
- » ¼ teaspoon freshly ground pepper
- » 1 red pepper-chopped, optional but a great addition

1. Heat the olive oil in a pot large enough to hold all the ingredients. Add the onion and sauté over medium heat until translucent. Add the garlic and sauté until soft but not brown.

2. Stir in the cumin and cook for two and three minutes. Add the squash, sweet potato, rutabaga, and turnip; stir to coat each piece with the onion garlic mixture.

3. Pour in the stock, being sure there is enough to cover the squash. Bring to a boil, turn down the heat and let it simmer for 30-40 minutes, or until the squash is very soft.

4. Puree the mixture using a blender or food processor. Thin the soup, if desired, with more stock. Add maple syrup, salt, pepper and red pepper to taste.

Garnish with chopped parsley, cilantro, or toasted pecans, or sunflower seeds.

Brunswick Stew

Versatile Favorite

- » 5 chicken breasts—cooked, shredded
- » 2 quarts (1.9 L) tomatoes
- » 3 cups (720 ml) chicken broth
- » 14 ounce (392 g) tomato sauce
- » 1 stick butter, omit if low fat is desired
- » 16 ounce (448 g) organic corn—frozen
- » 2 onions—chopped
- » ⅔ cup (150 ml) ketchup
- » 1 tablespoon vinegar
- » pepper—to taste
- » ⅓ cup (75 ml) Worcestershire sauce or Bragg's Liquid
- » Amino
- » 2 cups (470 ml) sweet creamy corn soup

1. *Combine all ingredients except chicken and corn. Cook on low in a crockpot 6-8 hours.*

2. *Add the rest of the ingredients right before serving.*

☞ *Flavorful Variations*

* This Brunswick stew can be made with any combination of pastas, beans, and vegetables. Variations are unlimited. Experiment and enjoy!
* Substitute corn soup with: any cream base soup including tomato, butternut squash, pumpkin or red pepper soup.

Classic Carrot Soup

- » 4 cups (960 ml) carrots, peeled and cut into 1" chunks
- » 2 tablespoons olive oil
- » 1 teaspoon salt
- » ½ teaspoon honey
- » ¼ teaspoon fresh ground black pepper
- » 4 cups (960 ml) water

Garnish:
- » 2 tablespoons fresh basil

1. *Preheat oven: 425°F (220°C).*

2. *Line large baking sheet with foil or parchment paper. Drizzle olive oil over carrots, stirring to coat well. Spread in a single layer on the baking sheet and roast them, stirring occasionally, for 25-30 minutes. Carrots are done when tender and lightly browned.*

3. *Place carrots, water, salt, honey, and pepper in medium saucepan and bring to simmer over medium heat. Reduce heat to low and continue to simmer for 5 minutes. Remove from heat. Blend with immersion blender* until completely smooth. Garnish with basil.*

* *May also be transferred to blender and pureed until smooth.*

4. *Roasting the carrots in the olive oil gives an additional depth of flavor and enhances the natural sweetness of the carrots.*

Corn Cheddar Chowder

» 1 tablespoon butter
» 1 cup (240 ml) chopped onion
» 2 tablespoons whole wheat flour
» 2 cups (470 ml) organic chicken broth
» 2 cups (470 ml) organic corn soup—in organic aisle
» 1 cup (240 ml) organic corn—whole kernel
» 1 cup (240 ml) brown rice—cooked
» ½ cup (120 ml) red pepper—finely diced
» ½ teaspoon hot pepper sauce
» 1 cup (240 ml) cheddar cheese
» Freshly ground black pepper

1. *Melt butter in a large saucepan over medium heat. Add onion. Cook and stir 5 minutes. Sprinkle onion with flour. Cook and stir 1 minute.*

2. *Add chicken broth, bring to boil, and stir frequently. Add corn soup, corn kernels, rice, bell pepper and pepper sauce.*

3. *Bring to a simmer. Cover and simmer for 15 minutes. Remove from heat and gradually stir in cheese until melted. Ladle into soup bowl and sprinkle with black pepper, if desired.*

Italian Vegetable Soup

- » 1 pound (454 g) ground turkey
- » 1 cup (240 ml) onion—diced
- » 1 cup (240 ml) celery—diced
- » 1 cup (240 ml) carrots—sliced
- » 2 garlic cloves—minced
- » 16 ounce (448 g) tomatoes
- » 15 ounce (420 g) tomato sauce
- » 15 ounce (420 g) red kidney beans
- » 2 cups (470 ml) chicken broth
- » 1 tablespoon dried parsley flakes
- » 1 teaspoon salt
- » ½ teaspoon oregano
- » ½ teaspoon sweet basil
- » ¼ teaspoon black pepper
- » 2 cups (470 ml) cabbage—shredded
- » 1 cup (240 ml) green beans—frozen
- » ½ cup (120 ml) elbow macaroni
- » Parmesan cheese

1. Brown turkey in a large heavy soup kettle and drain. Add all the ingredients except cabbage, green beans, macaroni and parmesan cheese.

2. Bring to a boil, lower heat, cover, and simmer for 20 minutes.

3. Add cabbage, green beans, and macaroni. Bring to a boil and simmer until vegetables are tender.

4. If you prefer a thinner soup, add additional water or broth. Sprinkle with parmesan cheese before serving if you like.

Lentil-Barley Stew

Tasty, Satisfying, and Economical

- » ¾ cup (180 ml) barley—hulled
- » 2 tablespoons olive oil
- » ¾ cup (180 ml) celery—chopped
- » ¾ cup (180 ml) onion—chopped
- » 6 cups (1.5 L) water
- » ¾ cup (180 ml) dry lentils
- » 1 quart (.95 L) tomatoes
- » 1½ teaspoons salt
- » ¼ teaspoon pepper
- » ½ teaspoon rosemary
- » 2 garlic cloves—minced
- » ½ cup (120 ml) carrots—shredded

1. *Soak barley overnight in water, then drain. Sauté oil, celery, and onion in pan. Add water and dry lentils.*

2. *Cook 20 minutes then add tomatoes, barley, salt, pepper, rosemary, and garlic. Simmer 45-60 minutes. Add carrots. Cook 5 minutes and serve.*

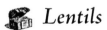 Lentils

Lentils, a small but nutritionally mighty member of the legume family, are a very good source of cholesterol-lowering fiber. Not only do lentils help lower cholesterol, they are of special benefit in managing blood-sugar disorders since their high fiber content prevents blood sugar levels from rising rapidly after a meal. But this is far from all lentils have to offer. Lentils also provide good to excellent amounts of six important minerals, two B-vitamins, and protein—all with virtually no fat.

Pumpkin Soup

» 3 tablespoons butter
» ¼ cup (60 ml) green pepper—chopped
» 1 small onion—finely chopped
» 1½ tablespoons whole wheat flour—soft pastry
» 1 teaspoon salt
» 2 cups (470 ml) chicken broth
» 2 cups (470 ml) low fat milk, heavy cream, or buttermilk
» ¼ teaspoon nutmeg
» 3 cups (720 ml) pumpkin—cooked
» ⅛ teaspoon thyme
» 1 teaspoon fresh parsley
» ½ teaspoon ginger

1. *Melt butter in a large pot. Add green pepper and onion to butter. Sauté until vegetables are tender.*

2. *Blend in flour and salt.*

3. *Add remaining ingredients and cook on medium heat, stirring constantly, until slightly thickened.*

3-Minute Cream of Chicken Soup

- » 4 cups (960 ml) water—boiling
- » 2 cups (470 ml) chicken broth
- » 1 cup (240 ml) white bean flour
- » 1 cup (240 ml) chicken—diced, optional

1. *In medium saucepan over medium heat, whisk bean flour into boiling water and add broth.*

2. *Stir and cook for 3 minutes. Blend for 1-2 minutes. Add chicken if desired.*

Makes 3-4 servings.

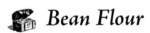 *Bean Flour*

Bean flours are a great way to make what you cook and bake more nutritious. Flour can be added to breads, casseroles and even desserts without the soaking, boiling, and waiting you think you need with beans. Bean flours can be added in small quantities to any baked goods without a change in flavor or texture. The addition of bean flour will make your breads a complete source of protein.
The flour can be made by grinding dry beans in your grain mill (Nutrimill).

Taco Soup

- » 2 pounds (908 g) ground beef or turkey—cooked
- » 2 cups (470 ml) onions— chopped
- » 2-15 ounce (420 g) cans kidney beans—rinsed
- » 2 cups (470 ml) organic corn— frozen
- » 14 ounce (392 g) tomatoes— diced
- » 1 small can black olives—sliced
- » 1¼ teaspoons taco seasoning mix
- » 2-15 ounce (420 g) cans pinto beans—rinsed
- » 14 ounce (392 g) Mexican tomatoes—organic
- » 14 ounce (392 g) tomatoes with chilies
- » ½ cup (120 ml) green olives
- » 1 ounce (28 g) Ranch Dressing Mix*

*see recipe in this book.

1. *Put all ingredients in a large stock pot. You may need to add some tomato sauce to add more liquid. Cook until heated.*

2. *Top with chips, sour cream, yo-cheese, cheddar cheese, or chopped onions.*

Tortilla Soup

- » 8 organic corn tortillas—stone ground
- » 8 teaspoons butter
- » ¼ cup (60 ml) butter—melted
- » 1 cup (240 ml) onion—chopped
- » 1 green pepper—cut in thin strips
- » 2 quarts (1.9 L) chicken broth
- » 28 ounce (784 g) fresh puréed tomatoes
- » 2 tablespoons Nature's Seasoning—or your favorite herb/salt blend
- » 1 cup (240 ml) cheddar cheese—grated
- » 1 large avocado—cut in wedges

1. *Preheat oven: 300°F (149°C).*

2. *Take 8 tortillas and butter each one with 1 teaspoon of butter. Cut the buttered tortillas into 3" strips, place on cookie sheets in single layer and bake until crisp for 20 minutes.*

3. *Place onion, melted butter and green pepper in a soup pot and sauté until tender. Add broth, tomatoes, and seasoning, bring to boil, reduce heat and simmer to blend flavors. Use cheese and avocado for topping. Garnish bowl of soup with cheese, avocado and tortilla strips.*

 *Avocado*

Avocados, typically grown in California, are a good addition to the meal. Choose one that is unblemished and heavy for its size. Place in paper bag to ripen in 2-4 days until it is soft to gentle pressure. Add the avocado to the dish at the last moment since it will discolor rapidly. This fruit is loaded with vitamins, minerals, healthy fats, protein and lots of phytonutrients.

Turkey Barley Soup

Ultimate Turkey Makover

- » 1 turkey carcass
- » 6 quarts (5.7 L) purified water
- » 12 peppercorns
- » 3 stalks celery—cut into fourths
- » 2 bay leaves
- » 1 large onion—cut into eighths
- » 1 garlic clove—minced
- » 1 cup (240 ml) barley
- » 2—16 ounce (448 g) cans tomatoes, drained and chopped
- » 1 medium onion—minced
- » 1 cup (240 ml) celery—chopped
- » 1 cup (240 ml) carrots—chopped
- » 2 teaspoons salt
- » ¼ teaspoon pepper

1. Combine first 7 ingredients in a large soup pot; bring to boil. Cover, reduce heat and simmer 1 hour. Remove carcass from broth, and pick meat from bones; set aside.

2. Measure 4 quarts (3.8 L) broth, and return it to soup pot; refrigerate remaining broth for other uses. Bring broth to a boil. Add barley; reduce heat to medium and cook 45 minutes. Add turkey, tomatoes, and remaining ingredients; simmer 30 minutes. Remove bay leaves.

Makes about 5 quarts (4.75 L).

Peppercorns

This spice was once so popular it was used for currency and determining trade routes. Peppercorns will stimulate digestive juices, thereby delivering a digestive bonus. Whole peppercorns freshly ground with a pepper mill deliver more flavor than the pre-ground peppers, which lose flavor after four months.

Garden Delight

Salads

Herbs and Spices

It is time to move our joy of food to the outdoors. Try your hand at growing your own herbs. Everyone will think you're a culinary whiz when you cook with fresh herbs from your garden.

EASIEST HERBS TO GROW

PERENNIAL

Thymes—English, Lemon
Oregano—spreads quickly
Sage
Rosemary
Russian Tarragon
Chives

ANNUAL

Basil
Dill
Parsley

DRIED VS. FRESH

Use 3 times more herbs if substituting fresh for dried

While dried herbs are convenient, they don't generally have the same purity of flavor as fresh herbs. To make sure the herbs are still fresh, check if they are green and not faded. Crush a few leaves to see if the aroma is still strong. Always store them in an airtight container away from light and heat.

Basil—Sweet, warm flavor with an aromatic odor. Use whole or ground. Good with lamb, fish, roast, stews, beef, vegetables, dressings, and omelets.

Bay Leaves—Pungent flavor. Use whole leaf but remove before serving. Good in vegetable dishes, stews, and pickles.

Caraway—Spicy taste and aromatic smell. Use in cakes, breads, soups, cheese, and sauerkraut.

Celery Seed—Strong taste which resembles the vegetable. Can be used sparingly in pickles and chutney, meat and fish dishes, salads, breads, marinades, dressings, and dips.

Chives—Sweet, mild flavor like that of an onion. Excellent in salads, fish, soup, and potatoes.

Cilantro—Use fresh. Excellent in salads, fish, chicken, rice, beans, and Mexican dishes.

Cinnamon—Sweet pungent flavor. Widely used in many sweet baked goods, chocolate dishes, cheesecakes, pickles, and hot drinks.

Coriander—Light lemony, orangey flavor. It is available whole or ground. Coriander is also called cilantro and can be used in apple pies and baked goods.

Curry Powder—Combining in proper proportion gives a distinct flavor to meat, poultry, fish, and vegetables.

Dill—Pungent aroma, used in pickling, salads, eggs, soups, seafood, and sauces.

Fennel—Sweet, hot flavor. Both seeds and leaves are used. Use in small quantities in pies and baked goods. Leaves can be boiled with fish.

Ginger—A pungent root, this aromatic spice is sold fresh, dried, or ground. Use in pickles, preserves, cakes, cookies, soups, and meat dishes.

Mace—Mace is the outer covering of nutmeg. Mace is a bit more delicate in flavor than nutmeg, but they can be used interchangeably. The warm, spicy-sweet taste is a frequent seasoning for baked goods and desserts. Mace will enhance meats, stews, and sauces as well.

Marjoram—May be used dried or green. Use to flavor fish, poultry, omelets, lamb, stuffing, and tomato juice.

Mint—Sweet cool aftertaste. Use in drinks, lamb sauce, fruit dishes, baking, and desserts.

Nutmeg—Whole or ground, sweet and spicy flavor. Use in drinks, puddings, soups, sauces, desserts, and pastas.

Oregano—Aromatic, slightly bitter. Use in tomato sauces, chili powder, barbecue sauces, soups, egg dishes, and cheese. Good with Italian and Mexican dishes.

Paprika—Pungent and peppery, but not hot. Use in meat, vegetables, and soups, or as a garnish.

Parsley—Mild flavor. Best when used fresh, but can be used dried. Use in fish, omelets, soup, meat, stuffing, and mixed greens.

Rosemary—Very aromatic. Can be used fresh or dried. Use in lamb, poultry, seafood, and vegetable dishes. Great in dressing.

Sage—Aromatic, slightly bitter. Use in stuffing, poultry, tomato juice, omelets, cheese spreads, and dressings.

Savory—This herb blends well with other herbs to make a salt-free seasoning that is good for stews, vegetable dishes, pizza toppings, roasting meats, and fish. By itself it adds flavor to bean dishes and evens helps with the digestion of beans.

Tarragon—Pungent, hot taste. Use to flavor sauces, salads, fish, poultry, tomatoes and eggs.

Thyme—Warm, slightly pungent, also lemon thyme. Sprinkle leaves on fish or poultry before broiling or baking. Throw a few sprigs directly on coals shortly before meat is finished grilling. Use thyme butter over vegetables.

Turmeric—Musky, slightly bitter, and peppery. Use in dressings, bread, soups, rice, noodles, and sauce.

Vanilla—Sweet and rich. Use in desserts, drinks, fruits, candies, and French toast. Only use natural, not imitation.

Black Bean Salad

» 1 cup (240 ml) black beans
» 1 cup (240 ml) organic corn kernels
» 1 cup (240 ml) red bell pepper—chopped
» 4 green onions—chopped
» ½ cup (120 ml) Italian dressing
» ¼ teaspoon onion powder
» ¼ teaspoon oregano
» ⅛ teaspoon garlic powder
» ⅛ teaspoon cayenne pepper

1. *Drain black beans and corn if canned or fresh. Add red bell pepper and green onions.*

2. *Mix seasoning ingredients with Italian dressing.*

3. *Mix all together and refrigerate.*

Curried Chicken Salad

» ¼ cup (60 ml) mayonnaise
» ½ cup (120 ml) yogurt—drained
» 1½ teaspoons curry powder
» 3½ cups (840 ml) chicken—cooked, shredded
» ½ cup (120 ml) celery—chopped
» 1 Granny Smith apple—chopped
» ½ cup (120 ml) raisins
» 2 green onions, finely chopped
» 1 teaspoon salt
» ½ cup (120 ml) walnuts—chopped

1. *Mix together mayonnaise, yogurt, curry powder, and then mix with chicken. Add remaining ingredients, saving walnuts until right before serving. Refrigerate.*

Serve with crackers, or it is great on pumpernickel.

If serving as sandwiches, it's great with a slice of tomato, lettuce, and a few sprouts.

Blackberry Mixed Salad

- » 8 cups (2 L) mixed salad greens
- » 1½ cups (360 ml) mango—sliced
- » 1½ cups (360 ml) pink grapefruit sections
- » 1 cup (240 ml) blackberries
- » 1 large avocado—sliced

Blackberry-basil vinaigrette dressing —See recipe

1. *Place salad greens and next 5 ingredients in a large bowl, and gently toss. Serve immediately with Blackberry-Basil Vinaigrette Dressing.*

Makes 6 servings.

 Tips for Selection and Care of Blackberries

Pick only ripe blackberries; these are black all over with no red drupelets. A gentle tug will release the blackberry from the stem. Handle blackberries gently; they are fragile. Blackberries will keep in the refrigerator for about two (2) days if they are unwashed and stored in an uncovered container. To freeze blackberries, simply put them unwashed in freezer containers, seal, and place in freezer.

Broccoli and Cauliflower Salad

Salad:
- » 1 head cauliflower
- » 1 bunch broccoli
- » 1 cup (240 ml) raisins
- » 12 strips turkey bacon—fried, crumbled
- » ½ cup (120 ml) cashews

Dressing:
- » ¾ cup (180 ml) safflower mayonnaise
- » ½ cup (120 ml) sucanat with honey
- » 2—tablespoons apple cider vinegar

1. *Wash and cut broccoli and cauliflower into bite size pieces. Add raisins, bacon, and cashews.*

2. *Do not add dressing until just before serving.*

〰 *Flavorful Variations*

* If cauliflower is not your vegetable of choice, you can change this recipe to 2 bunches of broccoli, 1 cup (240 ml) raisins, ¾ cup (180 ml) sunflower or pumpkin seeds, then add the dressing as suggested.

Fruit & Cinnamon Chicken Salad

- » 2 tablespoons onion—minced
- » 2 cups (470 ml) chicken—cubed
- » ½ cup (120 ml) celery—chopped
- » 2 tablespoons mayonnaise
- » 2 tablespoons yogurt
- » 1 cup (240 ml) grapes—sliced
- » ½ teaspoon cinnamon
- » ¼ teaspoon ginger
- » 1 cup (240 ml) pineapple tidbits—drained
- » ⅛ teaspoon salt

1. Mix all ingredients, adding sliced grapes right before serving. Refrigerate.

2. Serve with crackers, whole grain bread, or on top of salad greens.

 *Mayonnaise*

This thick, creamy dressing is an emulsion of oil, egg yolks, lemon juice or vinegar and seasonings. If yolks are not used it is a salad dressing. Homemade mayonnaise will taste superior to store bought and recipes can be found on the internet.

Curried Apple and Rice Salad

» 3 cups (720 ml) Near East Rice Pilaf—cooked
» 4 cups (960 ml) Granny Smith apples—chopped
» ½ cup (120 ml) walnuts—toasted
» 1 cup (240 ml) golden raisins
» ½ cup (120 ml) mayonnaise
» ½ cup (120 ml) yogurt
» 3 tablespoons lemon juice
» 1 tablespoon honey or orange marmalade
» ½ teaspoon salt
» 1 teaspoon curry powder
» 2 cups (470 ml) chicken—cooked, cubed, optional

1. In large salad bowl combine rice, apples, nuts, and raisins.

2. In small bowl blend mayonnaise, yogurt, lemon juice, honey, salt, and curry powder.

3. Pour over rice mixture, toss lightly, coating apples well. Serve as is or over a bed of greens.

 ## Curry Powder

Surprisingly, curry powder is actually a pulverized combination of 20 spices, herbs and seeds. Most commonly used are cardamom, chilis, cinnamon, cloves, coriander, cumin, fennel seed, fenugreek, mace, nutmeg, red and black pepper, poppy and sesame seeds, saffron, tamarind and turmeric (which gives it the yellow color). It will quickly lose its pungency and should be stored no more than 2 months.

Creamy Fruit Salad

- » 1-11ounce (308 g) can mandarin oranges—drained
- » 1 cup (240 ml) peaches—sliced
- » 1 cup (240 ml) pineapple chunks—drained
- » 4 ounce (112 g) cream cheese
- » ½ cup (120 ml) plain non fat yogurt
- » 2 tablespoons honey

1. *In a bowl, combine oranges, peaches, and pineapple. In a small mixing bowl, beat the cream cheese, yogurt and honey until smooth; pour over fruit and toss to coat.*

2. *Refrigerate for 15 minutes.*

Makes 4 servings.

 *Flavorful Variations*

* Optional ingredients can be added such as poppy seeds, nuts, and dried coconut.

Calypso Fruit Salad

- » 2 cups (470 ml) fresh pineapple cubes
- » 2 kiwi—peeled and sliced
- » 8 large strawberries—sliced
- » 1 cup (240 ml) fresh blueberries
- » 1-11ounce (308 g) can mandarin oranges—drained
- » 1 teaspoon lime peel—grated
- » ½ cup (120 ml) coconut—optional
- » 1 cup (240 ml) dairy sour cream or yogurt—drained
- » ¼ cup (60 ml) sucanat with honey or honey crystals

1. *In large bowl, combine pineapple, kiwi, strawberries, blueberries, oranges, and lime peel. Gently stir to mix.*

2. *Place coconut in glass pie plate. Stir fry on high for 1-1½ minutes, stirring every 30 seconds, until golden brown.*

3. *In small bowl, stir together sour cream or yogurt, and sucanat until sucanat dissolves.*

4. *Serve dressing alongside fruit. Sprinkle coconut over fruit. Garnish with fresh spearmint leaves.*

 ## Blueberry

Round and smooth-skinned blueberries are juicy and sweet. The season can span from the end of May to early October. Choose berries that are firm. Do not wash them until you are ready to use.

Cinnamon Pears

Very good side dish. The kids love it!

- » 4 Bosc pears
- » Juice of 1 lemon
- » 1 tablespoon sucanat with honey mixed with ¼ tablespoon cinnamon
- » 2 tablespoons water

1. Peel, quarter, and thinly slice each pear, one at a time, placing the slices at the bottom of a 6 inch saucepan. After the slices of each pear are layered, sprinkle some lemon juice and sugar-cinnamon mixture over the slices. When you reach the fourth pear, add the water then end with the remaining lemon juice and sugar cinnamon.

2. Cook over medium heat until boiling and then cover and continue cooking over a low flame until the pears are tender but not soft. Serve the pears lukewarm.

≈ Flavorful Variations

* Leftovers can be refrigerated and served at room temperature.
* This recipe is great topped with crumbled Earth Day bars.

Frozen Fruit Salad

- » 2 cups (470 ml) nonfat yogurt—vanilla or plain
- » ¼ cup (60 ml) honey
- » 4 ounce (112 g) lite cream cheese
- » 9 ounce (252 g) pineapple tidbits
- » ¼ cup (60 ml) pecans
- » 1 cup (240 ml) mandarin oranges—drained
- » 1 banana
- » 1 can whole berry cranberry sauce

1. Mix all ingredients. Freeze 4 hours.

Makes 10 servings.

 Wholesome Pecans

Fill a wide-mouthed quart (.95 L) jar with pecans. Add 1 tablespoon salt (Real salt preferred) and fill with water. Let soak at room temperature for 8-10 hours. Drain, spread nuts on a stainless steel pan, and dry in a warm oven, not over 150°F (65.6°C). Stir occasionally and dry until nice and crisp. Store in airtight container. Walnuts, peanuts, and almonds can also be used instead of pecans. Nuts that have been soaked, then dried, are easier to digest and their nutrients are more readily available.
* From Wholesome Sugar-free Cooking cookbook.

Cranberry, Feta, Spinach Salad

» Spinach leaves
» Feta cheese—crumbled, or goat cheese
» Craisins
» Walnuts—chopped, toasted
» ½ cup (120 ml) purple onions—sliced—optional

Use ingredients according to desired amounts.

1. Mix all ingredients except nuts. Toss with dressing at serving time.

2. Add toasted pecans or walnuts right before serving and stir.

3. This can be served warm or cold. Serve with Oriental Dressing or Cranberry Vinaigrette—See recipe under dressing section.

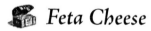 Feta Cheese

Feta cheese was originally made from raw goat's milk in Greece. Now it is commercially made from pasteurized cow's milk. Its fat content can range from 30-60 percent.

Fall Harvest Salad

Inventive Culinary Delight

Dressing

- » 4 green onions, chopped finely
- » 4 tablespoons olive oil
- » 2 teaspoons lemon juice
- » 4 teaspoons honey
- » 2 teaspoon Bragg's Liquid Aminos
- » ½ teaspoon salt
- » ¼ head cabbage, purple or green, shredded
- » 1 small raw sweet potato, shredded
- » ½ turnip—peeled and shredded
- » ½ cup (120 ml) unsweetened dried coconut
- » ½ cup (120 ml) raisins or currants
- » ¼ cup (60 ml) almonds

1. *Mix onions, olive oil, lemon juice, honey, liquid aminos, and salt. Stir until thoroughly mixed. Refrigerate until ready to add this dressing.*

2. *Combine cabbage, sweet potato, turnip, coconut, raisins and almonds. When ready add dressing.*

≈ Flavorful Variations

- * 1 cup (240 ml) raw beets—shredded
- * 1 cup (240 ml) jicama—shredded
- * 1 cup (240 ml) carrots—shredded
- * 1 cup (240 ml) rutabaga—shredded

Lentil Salad

- » 1 pound (454 g) lentils
- » 5 cups (1.4 L) water or broth
- » 2 teaspoons salt
- » 4 tablespoons olive oil
- » 1 large onion—finely chopped
- » 1 to 2 ribs celery—finely diced
- » ⅓ cup (75 ml) green pepper—chopped
- » ⅓ cup (75 ml) red pepper—chopped
- » ¼ cup (60 ml) pimiento—optional

Dressing:
- » ½ cup (120 ml) olive oil
- » 2 tablespoons wine vinegar
- » ⅔ teaspoon black pepper
- » 1 teaspoon salt

1. *Boil lentils in water or broth with salt. Reduce heat and simmer covered tightly for 28 minutes. The lentils should be tender, but still firm. Drain, toss with olive oil, and cool. Add onion, celery, pepper, and pimiento. Make the vinaigrette dressing. Pour over salad and toss well.*

Marinated Vegetable Salad

Superb and Beautiful to Serve

- » ½ cup (120 ml) safflower oil
- » ¾ cup (180 ml) cider vinegar
- » 2 tablespoons lemon juice
- » ½ teaspoon pepper
- » 1 green onion—thinly sliced
- » 1 garlic clove—minced
- » 1 tablespoon salt
- » ½ teaspoon oregano
- » ½ teaspoon dry mustard
- » 3 tablespoons honey
- » 2 cups (470 ml) zucchini—thinly sliced
- » 1 cup (240 ml) yellow squash—sliced
- » 1 cup (240 ml) broccoli florets
- » 1 cup (240 ml) cauliflower florets
- » ½ cup (120 ml) carrots—thinly sliced
- » ½ cup (120 ml) purple onion—chopped
- » 1 cup (240 ml) cherry tomatoes—halved

1. *Mix first 10 ingredients, shake well and pour over vegetable mixture. Marinate several hours before serving, even overnight, stirring occasionally. Beautiful and delicious.*

Navy Beans in Raspberry Vinaigrette

A combination that is irresistible—Serve as a vegetable or salad

- » 2 cups (470 ml) or one can drained navy beans or cannellini
- » 1 cup (240 ml) onion—finely chopped
- » 1 garlic clove—minced
- » 2 tablespoons parsley—finely chopped
- » 2 tablespoons fresh basil—chopped
- » 1 tablespoon fresh mint—chopped
- » ¾ teaspoon salt
- » Freshly ground pepper
- » 1 teaspoon honey
- » ¼ cup raspberry vinegar
- » ¼ cup (60 ml) olive oil
- » ½ cup (120 ml) fresh raspberries—rinsed and drained or frozen-thawed and drained

1. *In a 1-quart (.95 L) saucepan mix onion, garlic, parsley, basil, mint, salt, pepper, honey, vinegar, and olive oil. Mix well. Add the beans and mix lightly so as not to crush or break them. Heat over very low heat until warmed through. Serve warm or cooled. Just before serving gently stir in raspberries.*

Makes 4 servings

Mexican Frito Salad

» Romaine lettuce
» 15 ounces (420 g) of dark red kidney beans—rinsed, drained
» Black olives—sliced, rinsed
» Green onion—chopped
» 2 tomatoes—chopped
» 1 cup (240 ml) cheese—grated
» ½ pound (227 g) of seasoned ground meat—optional
» Corn chips—organic

Dressing:
» Russian, Honey Catalina, or Tomato Vinaigrette

1. *Place all ingredients, except chips, in a salad bowl. Toss with dressing and chips at serving time. Homemade dressings are great with this salad. Great with hamburgers and Mexican food.*

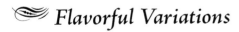 *Flavorful Variations*

* Season beef with onions, chili powder, and a touch of salt.

Mideast Pilaf

- » 1 teaspoon olive oil
- » 1 medium onion—chopped
- » 1 tablespoon sucanat or honey
- » ⅓ cup (75 ml) cashews or almond bits
- » ⅔ cup (150 ml) raisins
- » 3 cups (720 ml) brown rice—cooked, hot
- » 1 cup (240 ml) dried fruit (apple, apricot, etc.)—chopped
- » ¼ teaspoon salt
- » ¼ teaspoon ground cinnamon
- » ¼ teaspoon turmeric
- » ¼ teaspoon black pepper
- » ⅛ teaspoon cardamom
- » ⅛ teaspoon ground clove
- » ⅓ cup (75 ml) apple juice

1. In large skillet, heat oil and add onion and sucanat or honey. Cook for 3-5 minutes.

2. Add nuts and raisins. Cook for 2-3 minutes until nuts begin to brown and raisins are plump.

3. Add rice, dried fruit, and spices. Stir in apple juice. Serve immediately, or cold.

 ## Cardamom

Cardamom has a pungent aroma and a warm, spicy-sweet flavor. It can be purchased either in the pod or ground. Ground is more convenient but is not as full-flavored because cardamom seeds begin to lose their essential oils as soon as they are ground. Buying the seeds is best, and using a mortal and pestle makes quick work of the grinding. Be frugal when using cardamom—a little goes a long way.

Napa Mandarin Salad

- » 1 Napa cabbage—torn into 1" pieces
- » 1 bunch green onions—chopped
- » ⅛ cup (30 ml) soy sauce (Bragg's Liquid Amino)
- » ⅛ cup (30 ml) Bragg's apple cider vinegar
- » ⅛ cup (30 ml) olive oil
- » ¼ cup (60 ml) sucanat with honey
- » ½ stick butter
- » 1½ cups (360 ml) almonds
- » 1 cup (240 ml) chow mein noodles
- » 2 teaspoons sesame seeds
- » ½ cup (120 ml) sliced water chestnuts
- » 1 cup (240 ml) fresh snow peas
- » ½ cup (120 ml) chopped red pepper
- » 1 cup (240 ml) mandarin oranges, drained

1. *Finely shred the head of cabbage. Do not chop. Combine the green onions and cabbage in a large bowl, cover and refrigerate until ready to serve.*

2. *Dressing: In a small saucepan: add soy sauce, vinegar, oil, and sucanat, and bring to a boil. Let boil for 1 minute. Remove the pan from heat and let cool.*

3. *Stir fry the butter, almonds, noodles, and sesame seeds. Let cool or refrigerate for later use. When ready to serve, thoroughly mix dressing with water chestnuts, snow peas, and red pepper. Stir in cabbage and top with mandarin oranges.*

Orange Vidalia Sweet Onion Salad

Recipe from Georgia Vidalia Onion Growers Bland Farm

- » 6 oranges—sliced or chunked
- » 2 medium Vidalia onions—chopped, may sauté in oil to soften
- » 6 tablespoons olive oil
- » 3 tablespoons apple cider vinegar
- » 2 tablespoons honey
- » ½ garlic clove—minced
- » 1 tablespoon celery seed
- » 1 tablespoon basil
- » 1 teaspoon oregano
- » Mixed salad greens

1. Place oranges and onions in a large mixing bowl.

2. Prepare dressing by mixing together oil, vinegar, honey, garlic, celery seed, basil, and oregano.

3. Pour over oranges and onions and mix well. Chill. Serve on mixed salad greens.

Flavorful Variations

* You may also add other fruits such as blueberries, raspberries, etc. for a culinary delight.

Orange—Strawberry Salad

Wake up your salads with these pleasing fruits.

- » Romaine lettuce
- » Baby spinach
- » Organic greens
- » Green onions—sliced
- » Almonds—sliced, toasted
- » Strawberries—sliced
- » Oranges—sliced

Dressing:
- » ¼ cup (60 ml) olive oil
- » 2 tablespoons sucanat with honey
- » 2 tablespoons Bragg's Apple Cider Vinegar
- » ½ teaspoon salt
- » Dash hot sauce

1. *Mix dressing ingredients, shake well. Add dressing right before serving.*

When making fresh fruit salads, mix in some frozen seedless grapes just before serving. Everyone will comment on this clever, cool addition.

Spicy Cucumber Peanut Salad

- » 4 cups (960 ml) cucumber—peeled, halved, sliced
- » ¼ cup (60 ml) water
- » ¼ teaspoon red pepper—crushed
- » 2 teaspoons salt
- » ½ cup (120 ml) rice vinegar
- » 1½ tablespoons honey
- » ¼ cup (60 ml) red onion—slivered
- » 2 tablespoons peanuts—dry-roasted

1. *Combine first seven ingredients in a bowl. Let marinate at room temperature for at least 15 minutes. Sprinkle with peanuts.*

Quinoa: Basic Recipe

» 2 cups (470 ml) water
» 1 cup (240 ml) quinoa

1. *This light and wholesome grain may be prepared quickly and easily with this basic method. Rinse quinoa, either by using a mesh strainer or by running fresh water over the quinoa in a pot. Drain excess water. Place quinoa and water in a 1½ quart (1.4 L) saucepan and bring to a boil. Reduce to a simmer, cover and cook until all of the water is absorbed (about 15 minutes).*

2. *You will know that the quinoa is done when all the grains have turned from white to transparent, and the spiral-like germ has separated.*

Makes 3 cups (720 ml).

Read about Quinoa on page 107.

Quinoa Pilaf

- ¼ cup (60 ml) olive oil
- 2 garlic cloves—minced
- ½ cup (120 ml) carrot—diced
- ½ cup (120 ml) green onion—diced
- ¼ cup (60 ml) celery—diced
- ¼ cup (60 ml) green pepper—diced
- ¼ cup (60 ml) sweet red pepper—diced
- ½ cup (120 ml) mushrooms, chopped—optional
- ¼ teaspoon oregano
- salt to taste
- 6 cups (1.5 L) quinoa—cooked (see basic recipe)
- 1 cup (240 ml) almonds—sliced

1. *Sauté vegetables and garlic in olive oil until tender, yet crisp. Stir in oregano. Add sautéed vegetables to cooked, hot quinoa, mixing well. Add salt to taste.*

2. *Dry-roast almonds in heavy skillet until lightly golden.*

3. *Add almonds and mix.*

Apple Cranberry Quinoa

- » 2 tablespoons olive oil
- » ½ cup (120 ml) minced shallots, substitute green onions
- » ½ cup (120 ml) dried cranberries
- » ¼ cup (60 ml) maple syrup
- » 2 tablespoons fresh orange juice
- » 1 teaspoon cinnamon
- » Salt and pepper to taste
- » 3 cups (720 ml) quinoa—cooked—see recipe
- » 2-3 apples, peeled, cored and cubed

1. Combine olive oil, shallots, cranberries, syrup, juice, and cinnamon in a saucepan. Cover and cook over medium-low heat for 5 minutes.

2. Combine quinoa and apple in a separate bowl; stir until completely mixed, then add to cranberry mixture. Serve warm or cold.

Broccoli-Raisin Salad

- » 1 head broccoli—cut into bite size pieces
- » ½ purple onion—chopped
- » ½ cup (120 ml) raisins
- » ½ cup (120 ml) mayonnaise or yogurt
- » ¼ teaspoon Stevia or ¼ cup (60 ml) sucanat with honey
- » ¼ cup (60 ml) vinegar
- » 6 slices turkey bacon, fried crisp
- » ½ cup (120 ml) sunflower seeds
- » 2 hard boiled eggs, chopped, optional

1. *Combine broccoli, onions, and raisins. Make dressing with mayonnaise, stevia, and vinegar; pour over broccoli mix.*

2. *Store covered in refrigerator overnight. Just before serving, add sunflower seeds, egg, and crumbled bacon; stir into salad.*

Perfect Hard-Cooked Eggs

Purchase eggs (free range from a local farmer is best) at least one week in advance to make them easier to peel.

Place eggs in a saucepan that is large enough to hold them in a single layer. Cover with 1½ inches of cold water. Add a little salt to the water to set the egg white more quickly and seal any cracks that may occur. Bring water to a boil. Cover and turn off heat. Let stand for 15 minutes. Set timer to avoid overcooking the eggs. Rinse under cold running water for about 5 minutes to cool eggs quickly and avoid the grayish-green ring around the yolk. Store hard-cooked eggs in the refrigerator for up to one week. To determine whether an egg is raw or hard-cooked, place it on a table and spin it. Raw eggs will wobble and hard-cooked eggs will spin freely.

Jicama Slaw

- » 1 small head red cabbage—julienne style
- » 1 small head napa cabbage—julienne style
- » 4 medium carrots—grated
- » 2 medium or one large jicama—julienne style
- » ⅓ cup (75 ml) green onions—sliced
- » ¼ cup (60 ml) sunflower seeds—raw or toasted

Dressing:
- » ¾ cup (180 ml) apple cider vinegar
- » ½ cup (120 ml) yogurt—plain
- » 1 tablespoon Dijon mustard
- » 1 tablespoon honey
- » 2 tablespoons lemon juice or the juice of one lemon
- » 1 teaspoon salt
- » ⅓ cup (75 ml) olive oil
- » Poppy seeds—optional

1. Combine all ingredients for dressing and mix well.

2. In a large bowl, combine all the vegetables and toss until evenly mixed.

3. Add the dressing and mix well. Salt and pepper to taste. Top with sunflower seeds.

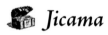 Jicama

This large, bulbous root vegetable with a thin brown skin and white, crunchy flesh comes from Mexico. It is good both raw and cooked. It should be stored in the refrigerator in a plastic bag and will last for about 2 weeks. It is loaded with vitamins and fiber. Makes a crunchy addition to any salad.

Salmon Salad

- » 4 cups (960 ml) salmon—cooked, chopped or canned wild
- » ½ cup (120 ml) nonfat yogurt
- » ½ cup (120 ml) mayonnaise
- » 2 tablespoons lemon juice
- » salt—to taste
- » pepper—to taste

1. *Prepare the salmon by grilling in oiled tin foil, broiling, or poaching in salted water. Cool and remove bones.*

2. *Mix all ingredients and refrigerate. Serve on crackers or as a sandwich. Great on whole wheat, pumpernickel, or rye bread.*

Flavorful Variations

* For optional flavors add chopped onions, pickles, red bell peppers, palmetto, plus whatever you may like.

Southwest Turkey Salad

- » tortilla chips
- » lettuce—shredded
- » 3 celery stalks—diced
- » 2 cups (470 ml) organic corn
- » 2 cups (470 ml) kidney beans—rinsed
- » 2 cups (470 ml) turkey—cubed
- » ⅔ cup (150 ml) salsa
- » ½ cup (120 ml) yogurt— drained
- » 1 teaspoon cumin
- » ¾ teaspoon salt
- » ½ teaspoon pepper

1. Layer tortilla chips, lettuce, celery, corn, beans, turkey. Mix remaining ingredients into a dressing. Top the layers with dressing.

Note: This can be prepared ahead of time and put together at the last minute.

Garlic Croutons

- » 2 garlic cloves—minced
- » 1 tablespoon water
- » 1 teaspoon olive oil
- » 5 slices whole grain bread— cubed
- » 1 teaspoon seasoning salt or Cajun seasoning

1. Preheat oven: 325°F (163°C).

2. Sauté garlic in water and oil. Add bread cubes, tossing to coat. Sprinkle with seasoning. Spread on baking sheet, and bake for approximately 15-20 minutes. Serve with favorite salad.

Spinach Salad with Poppy Seed Dressing

- » ½ cup (120 ml) sucanat with honey
- » 1 teaspoon dry mustard
- » ½ cup (120 ml) apple cider vinegar
- » 1 teaspoon celery salt
- » ½ cup (120 ml) honey
- » ⅔ cup (150 ml) olive oil
- » 1-2 teaspoons poppy seeds
- » spinach—torn into bite size pieces
- » bananas—sliced
- » strawberries—sliced
- » pineapple—sliced
- » walnuts—toasted

1. *Place spinach, fruit, and walnuts in a bowl and set to the side. Mix dressing ingredients with blender, food processor, or whisk. Add 1-2 teaspoons poppy seeds. Keep in refrigerator.*

2. *Bring to room temperature before using. Pour over salad (spinach, fruit, and walnuts).*

Flavorful Variations

* Use mandarin oranges instead of the fruit listed above. Use the same dressing and nuts.

Low Fat Fruit Salad with Poppy Seed Dressing

- » 1-8 ounce (224 g) can pineapple tidbits in unsweetened juice (reserve pineapple juice for later use)
- » 1½ cups (360 ml) strawberries or red grapes, halved
- » 1 medium apple—cut into bite size pieces
- » 1-10½ ounce (294 g) can mandarin orange sections—water pack, drained
- » ½ cup (120 ml) low-fat yogurt
- » ½ teaspoon poppy seeds
- » romaine lettuce leaves, washed

1. Drain pineapple, reserving 1 tablespoon of the juice.

2. For the fruit mixture, in a medium bowl, combine the pineapple, strawberries or grapes, apple and orange sections. Toss lightly to mix.

3. For dressing, combine yogurt, poppy seed, and the reserved pineapple juice.

4. To serve, line salad plates with the lettuce leaves. Arrange fruit mixture on the lettuce. Drizzle dressing over fruit.

Makes 6-8 servings.

Strawberry Spinach Salad

- » 2 tablespoons lemon juice
- » 2 tablespoons white wine or rice vinegar
- » 3 tablespoons honey
- » 1 tablespoon olive oil
- » 1 teaspoon poppy seeds
- » 6 ounces (168 g) baby spinach
- » ¼ red onion—sliced
- » ½ cup (120 ml) cucumber—sliced
- » 8 ounces (224 g) strawberries—sliced
- » ¼ cup (60 ml) almonds—sliced

1. *Prepare dressing with first five ingredients ahead of time. Refrigerate.*

2. *Mix with salad at serving time.*

 Purchasing fruits and vegetables

Buying fruits and vegetables for your salad is just as important as using the right recipe. Whenever possible buy organic, unbagged greens. Always wash the vegetables and fruits with a high quality organic cleaner and natural scrub brush.

Tabouli (Wheat Garden Salad)

- » ½ cup (120 ml) bulgur wheat
- » ¾ cup (180 ml) boiling water
- » 3 tablespoons olive oil
- » 2 tablespoons lemon juice
- » 1 teaspoon salt
- » ¼ teaspoon garlic powder
- » ½ teaspoon dried oregano leaves
- » pinch of allspice
- » 1 cucumber—seeded, diced
- » ¼ cup (60 ml) green onions—chopped
- » ½ cup (120 ml) fresh parsley—chopped
- » ¼ cup (60 ml) fresh mint—chopped
- » 1 large tomato—chopped

1. *In medium bowl, pour boiling water over bulgur wheat. Let sit 30 minutes.*

2. *Mix in shaker: oil, lemon juice, garlic powder, oregano and allspice. Mix wheat, vegetables, parsley and mint.*

3. *Pour in oil mixture and stir well.*

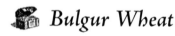 *Bulgur Wheat*

Bulgur wheat consists of wheat kernels that have been steamed, dried and crushed. It is often confused with, but is not exactly the same as cracked wheat. Bulgur has a tender chewy texture and comes in course, medium and fine grinds.

Tomatoes Stuffed with Chicken Salad

- » 6 large tomatoes
- » 2 cups (470 ml) chicken—cooked, cubed
- » ½ cup (120 ml) red bell pepper—minced
- » ½ cup (120 ml) frozen corn
- » 1½ tablespoons red onion—minced
- » 6 tablespoons olive oil
- » 1 tablespoon fresh parsley
- » 1 tablespoon mustard
- » 1 tablespoon yogurt
- » 1 teaspoon ground black pepper
- » ½ teaspoon salt
- » ¼ cup (60 ml) lemon juice
- » squirt lime juice
- » lettuce or spinach leaves

1. Cut ½ inch off the top of each tomato. Scoop out pulp from tomatoes. Turn tomatoes upside down on paper towels to drain.

2. In a medium bowl, combine chicken, bell pepper, corn, and onion.

3. In a small bowl whisk together olive oil and the next 7 ingredients. Pour this over chicken, tossing gently to coat.

4. Place tomatoes on lettuce or spinach leaves. Spoon chicken salad evenly into tomatoes.

5. Refrigerate or serve immediately.

Wild Rice Fruited Salad

Very versatile as a main dish, salad or dessert.

Dressing:
- » ½ cup (120 ml) orange or grape juice
- » 3 tablespoons olive oil
- » 2 tablespoons honey

Salad:
- » 1½ cup (360 ml) cooked wild rice
- » 2 golden delicious apples— chopped
- » Juice of 1 lemon
- » 1 cup (240 ml) raisins
- » 1 cup (240 ml) seedless red grapes—halved
- » 2 tablespoons each minced fresh mint, parsley, and chives
- » ⅓ cup (75 ml) pecans or walnuts—chopped
- » Pepper

1. Combine dressing ingredients; set aside.

2. Cook rice according to directions; drain and cool.

3. In a large bowl toss apples with lemon juice. Add raisins, grapes, mint, parsley, chives, and rice. Add dressing and toss. Season with pepper.

4. Cover and chill several hours or overnight. Just before serving, top with pecans.

Makes 10 servings.

 Wild Rice

Changing to wild rice may be a big step for your family, so this recipe is a good start. The added ingredients really give this dish an enjoyable flavor. Mixing in a little chicken broth when the rice is cooked will enhance the flavor even more. This is a great dish to prepare ahead of time for company, or just for family. It also makes a great luncheon main dish.

Wild rice is known for its nutty and flavorful chewy texture, but is not really rice at all. It is a long-grain marsh grass. It's important to clean wild rice thoroughly before cooking it. Wild rice is more expensive, but adding it to brown rice or bulgur wheat will extend your budget.

Winter Salad

Dressing:
- » ½ cup (120 ml) lemon juice
- » 1 tablespoon onion—finely diced
- » 2 teaspoons Dijon mustard
- » ½ teaspoon salt
- » 4 tablespoons canola oil
- » 6 tablespoons honey
- » 1 tablespoon poppy seeds

Salad:
- » Romaine lettuce—torn into bite size pieces
- » 4 ounces (112 g) lite cheese—Jarlsberg—diced
- » 1 cup (240 ml) cashews
- » ⅓ cup (75 ml) dried cranberries
- » 3 gala apples—cored, diced
- » 2 bosc pears—cored, diced

1. *Dressing: In a blender or small food processor combine lemon juice, onion, mustard, and salt. Process until well blended. With machine still running, add canola oil and honey in a slow, steady stream until mixture is thick and smooth. Add poppy seeds and process just a few seconds more to mix.*

2. *Salad: In a large serving bowl, toss together the romaine lettuce, cheese, cashews, cranberries, apples, and pears. Pour dressing over salad just before serving and toss to coat.*

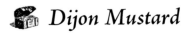 *Dijon Mustard*

Originally from Dijon, France, this pale grayish-yellow mustard is know for its clean, sharp flavor, which can range from mild to hot. It is made from brown or black mustard seeds, white wine, unfermented grape juice and various seasonings.

Zesty Rice and Bean Salad

- » 2 tablespoons olive oil
- » 1 garlic clove, chopped
- » ½ teaspoon ground red pepper
- » ¼ cup (60 ml) fresh lime juice
- » ¼ teaspoon salt
- » 2 cups (470 ml) brown rice—cooked
- » 15 ounce (420 g) black beans—rinsed, drained
- » 15 ounce (420 g) kidney beans, rinsed
- » ¼ cup (60 ml) feta cheese
- » 4 green onions, sliced
- » ¼ cup (60 ml) fresh mint—chopped
- » ¼ cup (60 ml) fresh cilantro—chopped

1. *Whisk together first five ingredients. Add the remaining ingredients to coat. Cover and chill one hour.*

✎ Flavorful Variations

* May substitute red onions instead of green onions.

Dressings

Famous Cover Ups

Salad Dressings

Freshness at its best comes with your own homemade dressings. Don't let this idea intimidate you. These recipes are very tasty and much more enjoyable than store bought. Store dressings usually contain MSG and other preservatives that are not healthy choices.

Craft stores carry a wide range of glass bottles perfect for your homemade dressings. Label all dressings with recipe name and date made. Homemade dressings are best used within 2-3 weeks.

Basic Vinaigrette

- » 1 cup (240 ml) olive oil
- » ½ cup (120 ml) red or white vinegar
- » 2 garlic cloves—minced
- » 3 tablespoons Parmesan cheese
- » 1 teaspoon Dijon mustard
- » ¼ teaspoon black pepper

1. *Place all ingredients in a blender, or just use a whisk. Mix and store in airtight glass container in refrigerator.*

Makes 2 cups (470 ml) of dressing.

Flavorful Variations

*   Substitute balsamic vinegar and add garlic or your favorite herbs.

Blackberry-Basil Vinaigrette

- » 1-10 ounce (280 g) jar seedless, sugarless blackberry preserves (make sure there is no artificial sweetener)
- » ¼ cup (60 ml) red wine vinegar
- » 1 tablespoon honey
- » 6 fresh basil leaves
- » 1 garlic clove—minced
- » ½ teaspoon salt
- » ½ teaspoon pepper
- » ¾ cup (180 ml) olive oil

1. *Pulse blackberry preserves, red wine vinegar and next 5 ingredients in a blender 2 or 3 times until blended. With blender running, pour olive oil through opening in the top in a slow steady stream. Process until smooth.*

Caesar Dressing

- » 2 tablespoons lemon juice
- » ½ cup (120 ml) sour cream
- » ½ cup (120 ml) mayonnaise
- » 1 teaspoon Dijon mustard
- » 2 garlic cloves
- » 2 teaspoons Worcestershire sauce
- » ⅛ teaspoon salt
- » ⅛ teaspoon pepper
- » 3 tablespoons olive oil

1. *Combine lemon juice and the rest of the ingredients, except oil. With blender running, gradually add olive oil in a slow, steady stream.*

2. *Refrigerate.*

Cranberry Vinaigrette

- » 3 tablespoons cranberry juice
- » 3 tablespoons olive oil
- » 1 tablespoon lemon juice
- » 1 tablespoon honey
- » 2 green onions—finely chopped
- » 2 garlic cloves—minced
- » 1 teaspoon dried oregano
- » ¼ teaspoon salt
- » ⅛ teaspoon pepper

1. *Mix all ingredients and toss on your favorite salad.*

Dill Dressing or Dip

- » 2 cups (470 ml) yo-cheese (or sour cream and mayo combination)
- » Handful walnuts—chopped, optional
- » 1 tablespoon fresh dill or more to taste—chopped
- » 1 tablespoon cilantro—chopped
- » Salt—to taste
- » 2 garlic cloves—minced

1. Mix all ingredients together.

Dill Dressing

- » ⅔ cup (150 ml) olive oil
- » ¼ cup (60 ml) red wine vinegar
- » 1 tablespoon sucanat with honey
- » 1 teaspoon salt
- » 1 teaspoon dill
- » ⅛ teaspoon curry powder
- » ⅛ teaspoon pepper

1. Mix all ingredients and cook over low heat for 2 minutes, stirring once.

Orange Dressing

- » ⅓ cup (75 ml) orange juice
- » 2 tablespoons balsamic vinegar
- » 2 tablespoons olive oil
- » 1 teaspoon honey

1. Whisk to combine all ingredients.

Oriental Salad Dressing

- » ½ cup (120 ml) olive oil
- » 1 tablespoon sesame seed oil
- » ½ cup (120 ml) apple cider vinegar
- » 2 tablespoons Bragg's Liquid Amino
- » 1 tablespoon fresh ginger
- » 2 tablespoons honey
- » 1 tablespoon sesame seeds

1. In medium bowl, whisk all ingredients together.

Refrigerate in dressing bottle.

Simple Italian Dressing

- » ¼ cup (60 ml) red wine vinegar
- » ½ cup (120 ml) water
- » ½ cup (120 ml) olive oil
- » 2 teaspoons Italian seasoning
- » 1 teaspoon honey
- » 1 teaspoon salt
- » 1 garlic clove crushed
- » 1 teaspoon onion, crushed
- » ¼ teaspoon ground black pepper

1. Place all ingredients in blender or use a whisk.

2. Blend for approximately 15 seconds. Refrigerate in a glass jar.

Makes 1½ cups of dressing.

Soy Ginger Sesame Dressing

- » ¾ cup (180 ml) nonfat yogurt—slightly drained
- » 1½ tablespoons Bragg's Liquid Amino
- » 3 tablespoons rice wine vinegar
- » 2 garlic cloves—minced
- » 1 tablespoon honey
- » 1 tablespoon sesame seeds

1. In a bowl, mix well and store to pour over salads.

Ranch Dressing Mix

- » 1½ teaspoons salt
- » 2 teaspoons parsley flakes
- » 1 teaspoon garlic powder
- » 1 teaspoon pepper
- » ½ teaspoon onion powder

1. *Mix these ingredients and store in refrigerator in airtight jar.*

❧ Flavorful Variations

* **Ranch Dressing:** 2 tablespoons of mix, 1 cup (240 ml) buttermilk and 1 cup (240 ml) yogurt.
* **Thousand Island Dressing:** To Ranch Dressing Mix add chili sauce and pickle relish.
* **Cucumber Dressing:** To Ranch Dressing Mix add ½ cucumber (peeled and chopped) and ½ teaspoon celery seed. Blend until smooth and refrigerate until cold.
* **Valley Ranch Dressing:** 31/8 teaspoons Ranch Dressing Mix, ½ cup (120 ml) lite safflower mayonnaise, ½ cup (120 ml) nonfat plain yogurt and 1 cup (240 ml) buttermilk. Combine all ingredients, mixing well. Refrigerate in airtight jar. Use within a week or two; check expiration date on yogurt. Serve with raw vegetables or as a dip.
* **Herb Dressing:** To Valley Ranch Dressing recipe, add ½ teaspoon tarragon and 1 tablespoon chopped chives to 1 pint (470 ml) Valley Ranch Dressing.
* **Dill Dressing:** To Valley Ranch Dressing recipe, add 1 tablespoon dill weed and a dash Worcestershire sauce to 1 pint (470 ml) of Valley Ranch Dressing.

Rhubarb Dressing

- » 2 cups (470 ml) fresh or frozen rhubarb—chopped
- » ½ cup (120 ml) sucanat with honey
- » ¼ cup (60 ml) apple cider vinegar
- » ¾ cup (180 ml) olive oil
- » 1½ teaspoons Worcestershire sauce
- » 3 tablespoons onion—grated
- » ½ teaspoon salt

1. In a saucepan, combine rhubarb, sucanat, and vinegar. Cook over medium heat until the rhubarb is tender, about 6 minutes.

2. Drain and reserve about 6 table-spoons of juice. Discard the pulp.

3. Pour juice into a jar with a tight-fitting lid. Add oil, Worcestershire sauce, onion, and salt. Shake well.

4. Refrigerate for at least 1 hour.

Tangy Sweet Russian Dressing

- » ¼ cup (60 ml) olive oil
- » ¼ cup (60 ml) honey
- » 2 tablespoons apple cider vinegar
- » ⅛ teaspoon dry mustard
- » 1 teaspoon ginger
- » ¼ cup (60 ml) safflower oil
- » ¼ cup (60 ml) catsup
- » 1½ teaspoons Bragg's Liquid Amino

1. Mix all ingredients in bowl with whisk. Store in an airtight bottle in the refrigerator.

Tarragon Vinaigrette Dressing or Marinade

- » ¼ cup (60 ml) white wine vinegar
- » 3 tablespoons olive oil
- » ¼ cup (60 ml) Worcestershire sauce
- » 1 tablespoon fresh tarragon
- » 1 tablespoon honey
- » ¼ teaspoon salt
- » ⅛ teaspoon pepper

1. Mix all ingredients together and chill.

2. Use as marinade for grilled vegetables, chicken or turkey.

Honey Mustard Vinaigrette

- » 3 tablespoons balsamic vinegar
- » 1 teaspoon salt
- » ¼ cup (60 ml) honey
- » 1 tablespoon Dijon mustard
- » 1½ tablespoon fresh parsley—chopped
- » ½ cup (120 ml) olive oil

1. Whisk together all ingredients except olive oil. Slowly drizzle in oil, whisking constantly until emulsified.

2. Refrigerate.

Zesty French Dressing

- » 1 small onion—minced
- » ⅔ cup (150 ml) olive oil
- » ½ cup (120 ml) sucanat with honey
- » ¼ cup (60 ml) apple cider vinegar
- » 2 tablespoons organic catsup
- » 1½ teaspoons Worcestershire sauce
- » 1½ teaspoons salt
- » 1 teaspoon mustard
- » 1 teaspoon paprika
- » 1 garlic clove—minced
- » ½ teaspoon celery seed

1. In a blender or food processor, process all ingredients until smooth and thickened.

2. Cover and refrigerate for at least 1 hour. Shake well before serving.

Carol's Herb Shaker

Great substitute for salt.

- » ½ teaspoon cayenne pepper
- » 1 teaspoon of each of the following: garlic powder, ground basil, marjoram, thyme, parsley, savory, mace, ground onion powder, black pepper, sage

1. *Mix together well. This recipe keeps for a long time. Very Good!*

Herb Shaker

- » 2 teaspoons **each:** garlic powder, onion powder, paprika, white pepper, dry mustard
- » 1 teaspoon **each:** powdered thyme, ground celery seed

1. *Mix together well. One shake enlivens salads, meat, poultry and vegetables.*

Give your guests something to chew on and freshen their breath at the same time. Herbal breath fresheners include basil, coriander, dill, peppermint, rosemary, sage, and spearmint.

Drink

to

your

Health

Adding Protein to Your Health Program

In the recipes that follow you will find many using protein as a main ingredient. There are basically 5 types of protein supplement powders on the market for five different reasons. All nutrition information mentioned below should be listed on the container.

1. **A Vegetable-Based (Soy) Supplement**—This is used primarily to add extra protein to your diet. A good soy protein drink is sweetened with fructose and glucose, both naturally occurring in fruits and vegetables. The essential amino acids should be listed on the can. This is a high protein, low fat health insurance.

2. **A Complete Meal Replacement**—Most of the time this is a nonfat, dry milk-based product. It should contain a full complement of vitamins and minerals for a complete meal replacement.

3. **A Weight Loss Supplement**—This is usually a protein mix of milk protein and soy protein isolate. It can be used as a meal replacement. Of all the protein supplements, the one for weight loss needs to be in perfect balance for your body. It should be powerful enough to be mixed with plain water in case you are not around cold milk. The drink should also contain a minimum of 4g of fiber. This will help you feel fuller longer. One serving in plain water should give about 15g protein, 3g of fat, and around 210 calories.

4. **Serious Athlete**—A good supplement would be a milk protein based product precisely designed and clinically tested to give faster energy return, increased muscle mass, and strength. This category would also include hard physical labor; recovery from surgery, injury or illness; yard work; garage cleanups; or physical therapy for neuron-muscular

disorders. In all these activities a good product can help you suffer less soreness, have better endurance, faster recovery, and more energy.

5. **A Work-Out Drink**—This should be a milk protein-based drink specifically designed for energy recovery and fuel for tired hungry muscles. This drink should contain 12g of protein, 33g carbohydrates, .5g fat and around 180 calories.

*** Be sure there is published science to back up the claims of the product. A lot of statements on muscle-building products are a sales pitch and pure hype. Look for a reputable company with a 100% guarantee.

What to Look For in a Good Protein Supplement

- It should contain no artificial sweeteners, flavors, preservatives, or colors. These do nothing for health.
- It should be a quality protein with a high level of biological availability. Under the FDA standard for assessing protein quality, the pattern of the nine essential amino acids in a protein is compared to the actual human requirements of these amino acids. Then an adjustment is applied based on how well the proteins are digested. Soy protein has been given a score of one, the highest possible rating, and is equal to animal proteins such as those from free range eggs and organic milk.
- Low in fat and should state a NON GMO.
- 99% lactose free.
- It should contain no hormones, antibiotics, or other dangerous chemicals.
- There should be minimal cholesterol.
- Preparation should be easy. It should mix in water, milk, or juice for convenience.
- Except for a muscle-building product, the supplement should be low enough in calories to be useful in weight reduction or in a weight maintenance program.
- There should be no superlative claims on the can or literature such as "lose weight while you sleep" or "massive muscles in 30 days" or other such statements.

Information gathered from: "Protein, A Consumer's Concern" by Bruce Miller, D.D.S., C.N.S, and Bruce Miller's Better Health Series.

Drink to Your Health

All drink recipes can be made in a blender with ice cubes. Frozen fruit makes the drink more like a smoothie. The protein used in each recipe is interchangeable: instant, vanilla, and chocolate, all soy based and non GMO (genetically modified).

If you are using Shaklee's premiere soy or whey products such as Cinch, Energizing Soy, Physique, and Instant—they can all be used interchangeably in these recipes. *See Resources for a list of suppliers.

Luau Mango Drink

Ingredients:
  » 4-6 ripe bananas
  » 2 ripe mangoes
  » 1 tablespoon honey
  » 3 ice cubes
  » ¼ cup (60 ml) apple juice or coconut milk

Preparation:

1. Blend all ingredients together until smooth. Serve in a tall glass.

Orange Julius

  » ½ cup (120 ml) orange juice
  » ½ cup (120 ml) milk (soy, rice, reg.)
  » 3 tablespoons soy protein powder
  » 2 teaspoons vanilla natural extract

1. Mix ingredients together. Enjoy!

Instant Protein Drink

- » 1 cup (240 ml) of your favorite fruit juice
- » ½ cup (120 ml) water
- » 1 serving instant protein powder
- » 1 teaspoon vanilla, almond or lemon flavoring

1. Mix together and pour in glass.

Pineapple Delight

- » ½ cup (120 ml) pineapple juice
- » ¾ cup (180 ml) cold water
- » 3 tablespoons soy protein powder
- » 1 teaspoon fresh lemon juice
- » Fresh pineapple—optional

1. Mix all ingredients together in blender.

Very Berry Drink

- » 4 strawberries
- » Several raspberries and blueberries
- » ½ banana—fresh or frozen
- » ¾ cup (180 ml) water
- » 3 tablespoons protein powder
- » ½ cup (120 ml) apple juice

1. Mix together in blender. A very tasty drink.

Tutti Fruity

- » ½ cup (120 ml) orange juice
- » ¾ cup (180 ml) water
- » Several berries—raspberries, blueberries
- » 3 tablespoons protein powder
- » ½ peach or nectarine
- » 2-3 strawberries
- » Almond or vanilla extract— optional

1. *Mix everything together in blender and pour in a glass. Makes 1-2 servings.*

Mystery Drink

- » ¾ cup (180 ml) water
- » ½ cup (120 ml) juice—your choice
- » 3 tablespoons protein powder
- » 2-3 tablespoons yogurt

1. *Mix ingredients together.*

Cranapple Flip

- » ½ cup (120 ml) cranapple juice
- » 2 tablespoons protein powder
- » ½ cup (120 ml) nonfat milk

1. *Blend with ice cubes.*

Fruit Smoothie

- » 2 cups (470 ml) nonfat plain yogurt
- » 1 banana
- » 1 cup (240 ml) red grapes
- » 1 apple—sliced
- » 8 strawberries
- » 1 cup (240 ml) blueberries
- » 1 cup (240 ml) ice
- » 1-2 tablespoons honey
- » 1 tablespoon flaxseed— optional, ground

1. *Blend on high and serve with straws. Any combination of fruit will do.*

Banana Smoothie

- » 1 banana—frozen
- » 1 teaspoon vanilla extract
- » 2 tablespoons protein powder—vanilla or cocoa
- » 8 ounces (224 g) milk
- » 1 tablespoon honey or other sweetener

1. *Blend with 6 ice cubes.*

Orangatang

- » ¾ cup (180 ml) cranberry juice
- » 2 tablespoons protein powder
- » ¾ cup (180 ml) orange juice

1. Blend with ice cubes.

Cocoa/Vanilla Treat

- » ¾ cup (180 ml) water
- » ½ cup (120 ml) milk (soy, rice, almond, reg.)
- » 3 tablespoons protein powder
- » 1 teaspoon vanilla extract
- » Dash of cinnamon

1. Blend all ingredients together.

Cocoa/Banana Smoothie

- » 3 tablespoons protein powder—chocolate
- » ½ banana
- » ½ cup (120 ml) milk
- » ½ cup (120 ml) water
- » 1 teaspoon vanilla extract

1. Blend all ingredients together.

Strawberry Cooler

- » ¼ cup (60 ml) strawberries
- » 2 tablespoons protein powder
- » 8 ounces (224 g) pineapple juice

1. Blend with 6 ice cubes.

Purple Delight

- » ¼ teaspoon lemon juice
- » 2 tablespoons protein powder
- » ½ cup (120 ml) grape juice
- » ½ cup (120 ml) lemon/lime soda

1. Blend with ice cubes.

Skinny Minnie

- » ½ cantaloupe or 2 cups (470 ml) cut up
- » 2 tablespoons protein powder
- » ⅓ can lemon/lime soda—your favorite

1. Blend with ice cubes.

Got Milk? Make Your Own

Processed milk is no longer the rich treasure it was designed to be. If your family would like options, consider making your own. No, I am not saying we all need our own cow, or to sign up for a cow share program; instead, we can get the richness of pure milk from the nuts and grains available to us daily. Here are some simple recipes to follow, and if your budget is tight the rice milk is very economical. When I first tried these recipes I was skeptical but quickly became thrilled with the simplicity and taste.

Almond Milk—Cashew Milk

» 1½ cups (360 ml) raw almonds or cashews
» 4 cups (1 liter) filtered or spring water
» ⅛ cup (30 ml) chopped dates-optional
» 1 teaspoon vanilla-optional

1. Soak almonds and dates in water for at least six hours.

2. Blend in a regular blender until you get a milk-like consistency. The dates add a hint of sweetness to your milk.

3. Strain once to remove almond granules, add vanilla.

The result is delicious, creamy milk that's free of added oils, concentrated sugars, and synthetic nutrients. This all-natural almond milk keeps for four to five days in an air-tight jar in the refrigerator.

If you have a Vita-mix, you can make almond milk easily.1 cup almonds and 3 cups water, agave or maple syrup to sweeten. To make it really creamy and nutritious, add some meat from a young coconut.

Almond Milk Shake

- » ½ cup (120 ml) vanilla almond milk—milk from recipe with ½ teaspoon or more of vanilla extract
- » ½ banana—can be frozen
- » 1 tablespoon agave nectar or honey
- » 1 tablespoon unsweetened cocoa powder
- » 1 scoop unflavored protein powder—I used a cocoa protein powder and omitted the cocoa powder
- » 4-5 ice cubes

1. *Blend everything until smooth. Very simple and tasty.*

Rice Milk

- » ½ cup cooked brown rice
- » 2 cups water
- » 1 tablespoon honey

1. *Blend in blender until smooth. This is a very economical option for making milk*

Rice Cashew Milk

- » 1 cup cooked rice
- » ½ cup cashews
- » 1 cup hot water
- » 4 cups cold water
- » Stevia and Vanilla optional

1. *Combine rice, cashews and hot water, Let sit for 10 minutes.*

2. *Add other ingredients; blend until smooth.*

Complimentary

Cookies

Are All Sweeteners the Same?

Eating is a pleasure, and since we have a portion of our tongue designated for tasting sweets, most of us don't want to leave these out of our diet. But are all sweeteners the same when we consume them? Reality teaches us that sweeteners come on a good and bad list when it comes to health.

To learn more detail about these sweeteners listed—both good and bad—read about them in the Treasure of Health Nutrition Manual.

Sweeteners to include in a healthy diet:

Sweeteners from natural sources given to us to please our taste buds in a delightful way.

Honey
Agave
Stevia/Truvia
Xylitol, Manitol, and Sorbital
Sucanat—all varieties

Sweetener alternatives to avoid:

Aspartame (NutraSweet/Equal)
Saccharin (Sweet N Low, Sugar Twin)
Acesulfame-K (Sunnett)
Sucralose (Splenda)
Alitame (Aclame)
Cyclamate
Neotame

Loaded Chocolate Oatmeal Cookies

Guaranteed to be a new favorite

- » ¼ cup (60 ml) butter—softened
- » ¾ cup sucanat with honey
- » 1 teaspoon ground cinnamon
- » ½ teaspoon baking soda
- » ⅛ teaspoon salt
- » 1 egg
- » 1 teaspoon vanilla
- » ¾ cup (180 ml) soft white pastry flour
- » ¾ cup (180 ml) old-fashioned oats
- » ¼ cup (60 ml) freshly ground flax seed
- » ¼ cup (60 ml) wheat germ
- » ½ cup (120 ml) dark chocolate chips
- » ¼ cup (60 ml) dried cranberries, raisins, or chopped dried cherries
- » ¼ cup (60 ml) chopped walnuts—toasted

1. *Preheat oven 350°F (180°C).*

2. *In a large mixing bowl, beat butter with an electric mixer on medium to high speed for 30 seconds. Add sucanat, cinnamon, baking soda, and salt. Beat until combined, scraping sides of bowl occasionally. Beat in egg and vanilla until combined. Beat in flour. Stir in old-fashioned oats, ground flax seed, wheat germ, chocolate, cranberries, and walnuts (dough will be a little crumbly).*

3. *Drop dough by rounded teaspoons 2 inches apart onto ungreased cookie sheets. Bake for 9 to 11 minutes or until tops are lightly browned. Let cookies cool on cookie sheet for 1 minute. Transfer cookies to wire rack to cool.*

Makes about 30 cookies

 ## Extracts

Always use pure extracts instead of imitation. Imitations are made from chemicals that do not build health. The pure extracts give a better flavor and may require lesser amounts.

Carrot Cookies

A delightful change of taste in a cookie

- » 1 cup (240 ml) organic butter—softened
- » 1½ cup (360 ml) sucanat with honey or honey crystals
- » 2 eggs
- » 1 teaspoon vanilla
- » 1 cup (240 ml) shredded carrots
- » 2 cups (470 ml) quick oats
- » 1¾ cup (420 ml) soft pastry flour
- » 1 teaspoon baking soda
- » 1 teaspoon salt
- » ½ cup (120 ml) walnuts—chopped
- » ½ cup (120 ml) raisins

1. Cream butter, sucanat, eggs, and vanilla until smooth. Add carrots.

2. Combine oats, flour, soda, and salt. Add to creamed mixture and mix well. Stir in nuts and raisins. Refrigerate 4 hours.

3. Preheat oven 375°F (190°C).

4. Grease cookie sheets. Bake 10-13 minutes.

Makes 3 dozen.

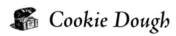 Cookie Dough

Unbaked cookie dough can be refrigerated for up to 2 weeks or frozen up to 6 weeks. It's convenient to have on hand when you want to bake up a batch in a hurry.

Chocolate Cherry Chews

- » ½ cup (120 ml) butter—softened
- » ½ cup (120 ml) sucanat
- » ¼ cup (60 ml) sucanat with honey
- » 1 egg
- » 1 teaspoon vanilla extract
- » ¾ cup (180 ml) soft pastry flour
- » ¼ cup (60 ml) cocoa, preferably Dutch processed
- » ½ teaspoon baking powder
- » ¼ heaping teaspoon ground mace
- » Dash salt
- » 1½ cups old-fashioned oats
- » ½ cup (120 ml) dark chocolate chips
- » ½ cup (120 ml) dried cherries—chopped finely

1. Preheat oven 375°F (190°C).

2. Lightly coat two baking sheets with non-stick spray.

3. In a large mixing bowl, cream together the butter and sucanat until light and fluffy. Beat in the egg and vanilla extract. Add the flour, cocoa, baking powder, mace, and salt; beat until smooth. Stir the oats, chocolate chips, and cherries into the dough by hand. Mixture will be very stiff.

4. Using about 1 tablespoon of dough, drop cookies onto prepared baking sheets about an inch apart. Bake 10-12 minutes or until the tops appear dry but not browned. Remove to a wire rack and cool completely. Store in an airtight container.

Makes about 25 cookies.

Easy Berry Oatmeal Squares

- » ¾ cup (180 ml) butter
- » 1 cup (240 ml) sucanat
- » 1½ cups (360 ml) soft wheat flour
- » 1 teaspoon baking soda
- » 1½ cups (360 ml) old-fashioned oats
- » ½ teaspoon salt
- » 1 8 ounce (224 g) jar 100% fruit preserves

1. Preheat oven: 375°F (190°C).

2. Cream together butter and sucanat. Mix dry ingredients together in separate bowl. Add dry ingredients to creamed butter and sucanat. Mix well. Spread half of mixture in 9" x 13" pan. Spread preserves over this layer and then put remaining mix over the preserves. Bake 20 minutes. Let cool completely and cut into squares.

Makes 20 squares.

Earth Day Bars

- » 1½ (360 ml) cups soft white pastry flour
- » 1 teaspoon baking powder
- » ½ teaspoon baking soda
- » 1½ cups (360 ml) quick oats
- » 1 cup (240 ml) sucanat
- » ½ cup (120 ml) butter
- » 1 egg
- » ½ teaspoon cinnamon
- » Optional ingredients: dried coconut, chocolate chips, raisins, or chopped nuts. One cup total of optional ingredients.

1. *Preheat oven to 350°F (180°C).*

2. *In a large mixing bowl, combine the flour, baking powder, baking soda, oats, sucanat, butter, egg, and cinnamon.*

3. *Stir the mix with a wooden spoon until you have a crumbly dough. Add optimal ingredients if desired, these ingredients will enhance the flavor of the bars.*

4. *Press the dough into an ungreased 9- by 13-inch pan and bake for 17 minutes, or until the center is set and the bars are slightly brown. Allow them to cool for 10 minutes before cutting.*

Makes 1½ dozen 2-by 3-inch bars.

 ## What is Earth Day?

It can be about celebrating the Earth in recognition of Who created it.
Psalm 24:1 The earth is the Lord's and all it contains.
Psalm 33:5 The earth is full of the loving-kindness of the Lord
Psalm 97:1 The Lord reigns, let the earth rejoice.

Healthy Banana Cookies

- » 3 ripe bananas
- » 1 cup (240 ml) raisins
- » 2 cups (470 ml) old-fashioned oats
- » ⅓ cup (75 ml) oil
- » 1 teaspoon vanilla

1. *Preheat oven: 350°F (180°C).*

2. *In large bowl, mash the bananas, stir in oats, raisins, oil and vanilla. Mix well and allow sitting for 15 minutes. Drop by teaspoons onto ungreased cookie sheet. Bake for 15-20 minutes.*

Makes 2 dozen cookies.

Instant Fudge

- » 1 cup (240 ml) protein powder
- » 1 cup (240 ml) natural peanut butter
- » ½ cup (120 ml) maple syrup or honey

1. *Mix thoroughly, press into pan and refrigerate until firm. Cut into bars.*

Flavorful Variations

* Add nuts, raisins, coconut, or chocolate chips.

Ginger Cookies

- ¾ cup (180 ml) butter—melted
- ¼ cup (60 ml) molasses
- 1 cup (240 ml) sucanat with honey
- 1 egg
- 3 cups (720 ml) soft white pastry flour
- 2 teaspoons baking soda
- 1¼ teaspoons cinnamon
- 1 teaspoon ginger
- ¾ teaspoon cloves

1. *Preheat oven: 350°F (180°C).*

2. *Cream butter, molasses, sucanat, and egg together. Beat well. Sift together flour, soda and spices. Add to creamed mixture. Use enough flour to create a good stiff cookie dough.*

3. *Roll into 1" size balls for cookies and place on cookie sheets. Bake for 10-12 minutes. Remove from oven and allow cooling on cookie sheet five minutes.*

Makes 5 dozen cookies.

Kids' Energy Bars

Perfect snack or light lunch

- » 1 cup (240 ml) natural peanut butter
- » ⅔ cup (150 ml) honey
- » 2 cups (470 ml) Nutty Flax Cereal
- » ⅔ cup (150 ml) chocolate soy protein
- » Chocolate chips

1. *Melt peanut butter with honey on the stove. Remove from heat. Stir in cereal and soy protein. Spread into 9 x 9" buttered pan.*

2. *Top this with melted chocolate chips. Refrigerate until firm.*

Makes 24 bars.

Nutty Flax Cereal is a cereal similar in texture to crispy rice but is loaded with fiber, typically found in the organic aisle. Other cereals can be sutbstituted. Look for 4 grams of fiber per serving plus a good crunch.

This bar is packed with nutrition, such as protein and fiber, but remember it has 127 calories per bar.

 ## Soy

Soy is a natural product that is a complete protein. Our bodies need protein every day to build healthy cells. The soy products on the market aren't always tasty, and most soy products are genetically modified. The wellness company known as the Shaklee Corporation, (#1 natural nutrition company in the U.S.) has an all-natural source of soy protein that can be used as a drink or added into all cooking. This recipe, and the No Bake Peanut Butter Bars, include a good supply of fiber and soy for a healthy diet.

No Bake Peanut Butter Bars

- » ⅔ cup (150 ml) protein powder
- » 1 cup (240 ml) quick oats
- » 1½ cups (360 ml) Nutty Flax Cereal
- » ¾ cup (180 ml) honey
- » 1 cup (240 ml) natural peanut butter
- » 2½ teaspoons vanilla
- » ⅔ cup (150 ml) chocolate chips

1. *Combine oats, protein, and cereal in large bowl and set aside. Bring honey to a boil on stove top. Remove from heat and stir in peanut butter and vanilla until smooth. Immediately add honey mixture to dry mixture until well mixed.*

2. *Stir in chocolate chips and press into 8" x 8" pan. Refrigerate 20-25 minutes until firm.*

Makes 12 bars.

Shaklee Instant Soy Protein or Energizing Cocoa Protein work well for this recipe.

No Bake Peanut Butter Cocoa Oatmeal Cookies

- » 1 cup (240 ml) honey
- » 1 stick butter
- » ½ cup (120 ml) milk
- » ½ cup (120 ml) cocoa
- » 1 teaspoon vanilla
- » 3 tablespoons natural peanut butter
- » 2 cups (470 ml) quick oatmeal
- » Nuts—finely chopped

1. Bring honey, butter, milk, and cocoa to a boil for two minutes. Add vanilla, peanut butter, and oatmeal. Mix and add nuts. Drop by rounded teaspoon on wax paper lined dish. Layer wax paper as needed. Refrigerate.

2. These are good frozen. Take out 5-10 minutes before serving

Makes 2 dozen cookies.

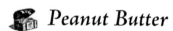 *Peanut Butter*

There are two good choices for peanut butter. The first is to grind your own from fresh organic peanuts in a health food store. The second is to buy peanut butter that has only two ingredients on the label: peanuts and salt. Besides these two choices, the other products will cause more harm to your body with the added fat and additives. Be a wise shopper.

Oatmeal Cookies

- » 1 cup (240 ml) butter—softened
- » 1 cup (240 ml) sucanat—any variety
- » 2 eggs
- » 1 teaspoon vanilla
- » 1½ cup (360 ml) soft white pastry flour
- » 1 teaspoon baking soda
- » 1 teaspoon cinnamon
- » ½ teaspoon salt
- » 3 cup (720 ml) quick oats
- » ½ cup (120 ml) flax seed—ground
- » 1 cup (240 ml) raisins, dried cranberries or chocolate chips (optional)

1. Preheat oven: 350°F (180°C).

2. Beat together butter and sucanat until creamy. Add eggs and vanilla. Beat well. Add combined flour, baking soda, cinnamon, and salt.

3. Mix well. Stir in oats, flax seed, and optional ingredients.

4. Drop by rounded tablespoons onto ungreased cookie sheet.

5. Bake 10-12 minutes. Cool 1 minute. Remove to wire rack.

Makes 4 dozen cookies.

Pantry Cookies

Versatile + easy + economical = a great treasure.

» 2 cups (470 ml) old-fashioned oats
» 1 cup (240 ml) honey crystals
» 1¼ cup (300 ml) soft white pastry flour
» ¼ teaspoon salt
» 1 teaspoon baking soda
» ½ teaspoon baking powder
» 1 teaspoon vanilla
» 1 stick melted butter
» ¼ cup (60 ml) hot water

1. Preheat oven: 350°F (180°C).

2. Combine oats, honey crystals, flour, salt, baking powder and baking soda. Add hot water, stir in vanilla and butter. Spoon dough on greased cookie sheets.

3. Bake for 10 minutes or until golden brown.

〰 *Flavorful Variations*

* Replace vanilla extract with almond extract and add ½ cup (120 ml) dried cranberries. ½ cup (120 ml) chopped almonds can also be added. These are a holiday favorite.

Peanut Butter Cookies

- » ½ cup (120 ml) natural peanut butter
- » ½ cup (120 ml) butter
- » 1 cup (240 ml) sucanat or sucanat with honey
- » 1 egg
- » ½ teaspoon vanilla
- » 1¼ cups (300 ml) hard whole wheat flour
- » ¾ teaspoon baking soda
- » ¼ teaspoon salt
- » 1 cup (240 ml) chocolate chips—optional

1. Preheat oven: 375°F (190°C).

2. Thoroughly cream together butter, peanut butter, sucanat, eggs, and vanilla. Sift together dry ingredients. Blend into creamed mixture and add chocolate chips.

3. Shape into 1 inch balls. Place 2 inches apart on ungreased cookie sheet. Press top in a crisscross pattern with a fork.

4. Bake for 10-12 minutes. Cool on cookie sheet.

Makes 3 dozen cookies.

Whole Wheat Snickerdoodles

Dough freezes well for long time enjoyment.

- » 2⅔ cups (620 ml) whole wheat flour
- » 1 teaspoon cream of tartar
- » 1 teaspoon baking soda
- » ½ teaspoon cinnamon
- » 1 cup (240 ml) butter
- » ⅔ cup (150 ml) maple syrup
- » 2 eggs
- » 2 tablespoons sucanat— powdered
- » 1 teaspoon cinnamon

1. *Preheat oven: 375°F (190°C).*

2. *Mix first four dry ingredients together in a small bowl. In a different, large bowl, cream butter thoroughly. Slowly add maple syrup to butter, mixing thoroughly. Mix in eggs, one at a time, to butter mixture. Add flour gradually and mix together.*

3. *Cover and refrigerate dough for at least one hour or until dough is firm enough to handle.*

4. *Form dough into 1 inch balls. Roll in a mixture of the 2 tablespoons of sucanat and cinnamon. Place on very lightly greased cookie sheet; flatten cookies slightly with bottom of a drinking glass.*

5. *Bake for about 8 minutes or until light golden. Cool on wire rack.*

Makes 5 dozen cookies.

Stella's Special Candy

- » ½ cup (120 ml) honey
- » ½ cup (120 ml) natural peanut butter
- » 1 teaspoon vanilla
- » 1¾ cups (420 ml) dry milk
- » Pinch of salt
- » ¼ cup (60 ml) unsweetened apple juice
- » 1 cup (240 ml) walnuts—chopped
- » 1 cup (240 ml) coconut—grated
- » 1 cup (240 ml) sesame seeds—optional

1. *Blend honey, peanut butter, vanilla, dry milk, salt, and apple juice together. Press onto flat surface and cut or roll into balls.*

2. *Coat with chopped nuts, seeds, or coconut.*

Taste and See
That the Lord
is Good

Happy Endings

Apple Crisp

- » 6 cups (1.5 L) apple slices— peeled
- » ¼ cup (60 ml) water
- » ¾ cup (180 ml) whole wheat flour or oat flour (ground oats)
- » 1 teaspoon cinnamon
- » ⅓ cup (75 ml) quick oats
- » 1 cup (240 ml) sucanat with honey or honey crystals
- » ⅓ cup (75 ml) butter

1. *Preheat oven: 350°F (180°C).*

2. *Place apples in a 10" x 6" baking dish. Add water. Combine flour, cinnamon, oats and sucanat. Using 2 knives or a pastry blender, cut in butter until mixture resembles coarse crumbs. Sprinkle over apples.*

3. *Bake for 40 minutes or until apples are tender.*

Makes 6 servings.

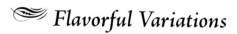 *Flavorful Variations*

*   Add chopped nuts and/or chopped cranberries

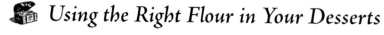 *Using the Right Flour in Your Desserts*

Most desserts will use the soft pastry wheat grain for the whole wheat in recipes. Whenever there is no yeast in the recipe, soft pastry is the flour to use. Hard white flour can definitely be used also and will create a good tasting dessert.

Harvest Pear Crisp

This dessert is a great change from apple.

- » ½ cup (120 ml) whole wheat flour
- » ½ cup (120 ml) sucanat, natural
- » ½ teaspoon (120 ml) cinnamon
- » ¼ teaspoon salt
- » ½ cup (120 ml) butter, cut into small cubes, chilled
- » 1 cup (240 ml) old-fashioned oats
- » ½ cup (120 ml) chopped nuts
- » ¼ teaspoon ginger
- » ½ cup (120 ml) sucanat, honey crystals
- » 2 tablespoon organic cornstarch
- » ½ teaspoon cinnamon
- » ¼ teaspoon salt
- » 4 pounds (1.8 kg) firm but ripe pears, peeled, cored, and cut into slices—about 6 cups (1.5 L)

1. *Preheat oven to 350°F (180°C).*

2. *Combine first four ingredients: flour, sucanat, cinnamon, and salt. Add butter and cut in. Stir in oats, nuts, and ginger. Stir until crumbly. Set topping aside in refrigerator.*

3. *Mix sucanat, cornstarch, cinnamon, and salt until thoroughly mixed. Add pears and toss to coat. Put coated pears in 13" x 9" pan and sprinkle topping over pear mixture.*

4. *Bake about 50 minutes until topping is crisp and golden brown and juices are bubbling. Serve warm.*

   Other fruits work well in this recipe.

Deep Dish Apple Pie

Prepare a crust using the whole wheat pastry recipe in this book or a favorite of your own.

- » 8 cups (2 L) apples—sliced thinly
- » ¼ cup (60 ml) sucanat with honey
- » ⅓ cup (75 ml) whole wheat flour
- » 1 teaspoon ground cinnamon
- » ½ teaspoon allspice
- » ½ teaspoon salt

Crumbly Topping:
- » ½ cup (120 ml) sucanat
- » ½ cup (120 ml) quick oats
- » ½ cup (120 ml) whole wheat flour
- » 1 teaspoon cinnamon
- » ½ teaspoon nutmeg
- » ¼ cup (60 ml) butter

1. Preheat oven: 375°F (190°C).

2. Mix together dry ingredients. Add apples and coat with dry mix. Put into pie crusts.

3. Stir together sucanat, oats, flour, cinnamon and nutmeg. Cut in butter until crumbly. Sprinkle over apple mixture.

4. Bake uncovered in a 9" x 13" pan for 30-35 minutes or until apples are tender.

Baby Heath Bars

Special Treat for Special Occasions

- » 4 cups (960 ml) oatmeal—uncooked
- » 1 cup (240 ml) sucanat with honey
- » ¼ cup (60 ml) honey
- » ¾ cup (180 ml) natural peanut butter—crunchy
- » 1 teaspoon vanilla
- » ¾ cup (180 ml) butter—softened

Topping:
- » 6 ounces (168 g) chocolate chips
- » 6 ounces (168 g) butterscotch chips
- » 1 cup (240 ml) peanut butter

1. *Preheat oven: 400°F (200°C).*

2. *Combine first 6 ingredients and spread in greased 9" x 13" pan. Bake in oven 12 minutes.*

3. *Melt chocolate chips, butterscotch chips, and peanut butter. Spread over bars after removed from oven.*

4. *Let cool. Refrigerate and cut into squares.*

   Makes 12 servings.

After-School Treat

- » 1 scoop ice cream
- » 1 tablespoon protein
- » ½ cup (120 ml) nonfat milk

1. *Blend together and serve.*

Lillie Peach Pops

Perfect Grandchild Treat

- » 16 ounces (448 g) unsweetened peaches—drained
- » 8 ounce (224 g) plain yogurt
- » ¼ cup (60 ml) protein

1. Blend peaches until smooth. Add yogurt and protein and blend again. Place in small paper cups or popsicle molds. Place wooden stick in center of each; freeze until firm. Other fruits would taste great also.

Pineapple Sherbet

Refreshing

- » 1 quart (.95 L) plain kefir—can substitute buttermilk
- » 1 can-20 ounce (560 g) crushed pineapple—drained
- » 1⅓ cups (315 ml) sucanat with honey
- » 1 teaspoon vanilla
- » Fresh pineapple slices—optional for garnish

1. In a bowl, combine the first four ingredients and mix well. Cover and freeze for 1 hour. Stir and return to freezer for at least 2 hours before serving.

Banana Cake

- » 1 stick butter
- » ¾ cup (180 ml) mild honey
- » 3 eggs
- » 3 bananas—mashed
- » 2 teaspoons vanilla
- » 1 cup (240 ml) nonfat plain yogurt
- » 2½ cups (590 ml) whole wheat flour—soft pastry or hard
- » 1 teaspoon baking soda
- » 2 teaspoons baking powder
- » ¼ teaspoon salt
- » ½ cup (120 ml) pecans—chopped, or chocolate chips

Frosting:
- » ½ stick butter
- » 6 ounces (168 g) cream cheese
- » ⅓ cup (75 ml) honey
- » 2 teaspoons vanilla

1. *Preheat oven: 325°F (163°C).*

2. *Cream together butter, honey, eggs, bananas, vanilla, and yogurt. Add creamed mixture to dry ingredients and beat well. Pour into a greased 9" x 13" pan.*

3. *Bake for 25 minutes. Let cool.*

4. *Cream frosting and whip until fluffy. Spread on cooled cake. Sprinkle a few chopped pecans on top.*

Makes 12 servings.

Banana Nut Cake

- » 3 cups (720 ml) whole wheat flour—soft pastry
- » 2 cups (470 ml) sucanat with honey
- » 1 teaspoon baking soda
- » 1 teaspoon baking powder
- » 1 teaspoon cinnamon
- » ½ teaspoon salt
- » 3 eggs—beaten
- » ¾ cup (180 ml) olive oil
- » 4 large ripe bananas—mashed
- » 1½ teaspoons vanilla
- » 1 cup (240 ml) pecans—chopped

1. *Preheat oven: 350°F (180°C).*

2. *Mix dry ingredients, set aside. Cream eggs, oil, bananas, and vanilla. Add to dry ingredients. Stir in pecans.*

3. *Bake in 13" x 9" pan for 23-28 minutes.*

This cake works well using round cake pans layered with frosting.

Chocolate Cloud

- » ½ cup (120 ml) whipping cream
- » ¼ teaspoon vanilla extract
- » ½ teaspoon stevia
- » 1 teaspoon unsweetened dark cocoa powder

1. *Whip cream, vanilla, and stevia in a bowl until stiff peaks form. Stir in cocoa with a spoon. Makes 2 servings.*

Stevia or Truvia

Stevia is a natural herb that can be found in most grocery or health food stores. It can be found in liquid or powder and is 100 times sweeter than sugar with no calories.

Carrot Cake

- » 3 eggs—beaten
- » ½ cup (120 ml) honey
- » ¼ cup (60 ml) buttermilk or yogurt
- » 1 teaspoon vanilla
- » ¾ cup (180 ml) organic canola oil
- » 2 cups (470 ml) grated carrots
- » ½ cup (120 ml) pecans—chopped
- » 1½ cups (360 ml) whole wheat flour—soft pastry
- » ½ teaspoon salt
- » 1 teaspoon baking soda
- » 1 teaspoon baking powder
- » 1 tablespoon cinnamon

1. Preheat oven: 350°F (180°C).

2. Blend first seven ingredients with a mixer.

3. Combine dry ingredients in a separate bowl. Fold dry ingredients into wet.

4. Pour into a greased 8" x 8" greased pan.

5. Bake for 45 minutes to one hour. Ice with your favorite cream cheese or yo-Cheese icing.

Cream Cheese Icing
- » 1-8 ounce (224 g) cream cheese (Neufchatel)—softened
- » 2 teaspoons vanilla
- » 2 tablespoons honey

1. In mixer, beat all ingredients until smooth. Spread on cooled cake. Refrigerate.

Surprise Brownies

Throw away the box mixes—this is better than you can imagine.

- » 1¾ cup (420 ml) pastry flour
- » ½ cup (120 ml) cocoa
- » ½ teaspoon baking soda
- » ½ teaspoon salt
- » 2 cups ((480ml) shredded zucchini
- » 1 cup (240 ml) shredded carrots
- » 1 egg
- » 1 cup (240 ml) sucanat with honey (honey crystals)
- » ½ cup (120 ml) sucanat natural
- » ½ cup (120 ml) fat free yogurt
- » 3 tablespoons butter
- » 1 teaspoon vanilla
- » ⅓ cup (80 ml) applesauce

Optional Toppings:
- » ½ cup dark chocolate chips
- » ½ cup nuts—chopped

1. Preheat oven: 350°F (180°C).

2. In large bowl combine flour, cocoa, baking soda and salt. Stir in zuchinni and carrots. In second bowl combine egg, both sucanats, yogurt, butter, vanilla and applesauce. Mix well and add into zucchini mixture. Spread in greased 9x13 pan.

3. Sprinkle ½ cup dark chocolate chips and ½ cup chopped nuts on top of batter.

4. Bake for 35-40 minutes.

Dried Fruit Balls

- » 1 cup (240 ml) dried apricots
- » ½ cup (120 ml) raisins
- » ½ cup (120 ml) pitted prunes
- » ½ cup (120 ml) unsweetened pitted dates
- » 1 cup (240 ml) pecans or walnuts—finely chopped
- » ½ cup (120 ml) unsweetened flaked coconut
- » ½ teaspoon fresh organic orange peel—grated
- » ¼ cup (60 ml) juice from one orange

1. *In a food processor, grind the dried fruits. Add half of the nuts, coconut, orange peel, and orange juice. Mix well and form into balls. Roll in remaining nuts.*

Makes 4 dozen.

Flavorful Variations

* These are excellent to keep in the freezer and pull out when you're craving something sweet. Dried fruit is packed full of nutrients. A great treat for a brunch, shower, gift, or holidays. This recipe is not recommended to be prepared in a blender.

Fresh Apple Cake

- » 2 cups (470 ml) whole wheat flour—soft pastry
- » 2 teaspoons cinnamon
- » 2 teaspoons baking soda
- » 1 teaspoon salt
- » 2 eggs—beaten
- » ½ cup (120 ml) olive or canola oil
- » 1 cup (240 ml) sucanat with honey
- » 2 teaspoons vanilla extract
- » 1 cup (240 ml) walnuts—chopped
- » 4 cups apples—finely chopped, peeled

1. *Preheat oven: 325°F (163°C).*

2. *Mix flour, cinnamon, baking soda, and salt. Set aside.*

3. *Blend together eggs, oil, sucanat, vanilla, and walnuts in a large mixing bowl. Fold liquid ingredients into dry ingredients. Add apples.*

4. *Pour into a Bundt pan and bake for 50 to 60 minutes, until knife inserted comes out clean. Allow to cool 10 minutes before removing from pan.*

Fresh Fruit Dip

- » 1-8 ounce (224 g) can coconut milk
- » Honey or sucanat—sweeten to taste

1. *Mix the milk with the honey or sucanat to the taste you desire. Refrigerate to make it cold and thicker.*

This is a delicious dip for fruit or as an icing to drizzle over brownies. A healthy alternative to marshmallow crème.

Granola Crunchies

- » 2 cups (470 ml) granola
- » ½ cup (120 ml) peanut butter
- » 2 tablespoons honey
- » 1½ teaspoon vanilla
- » Pinch of salt
- » 1 cup (240 ml) finely shredded coconut or 1 cup (240 ml) finely chopped nuts

1. *Mix all ingredients together with hands, except coconut or nuts, until well mixed. Form into balls, dipping hands in water, if necessary. Roll in coconut or nuts and freeze.*

Makes 2 dozen crunchies.

Fruity Ice Cream

- » 16 ounce (448 g) frozen fruit
- » ⅔ cup (150 ml) honey
- » ⅓ cup (75 ml) old-fashioned oats
- » 1½ teaspoons vanilla
- » 1 pint (470 ml) whipping cream

1. *Blend all ingredients in food processor or blender adding whipping cream or half & half until creamy.*

Flavorful Variations

* May use fresh fruit and ice cubes instead of frozen fruit. This dessert is quick and easy. It can be prepared in less than 5 minutes and served right away for an after-dinner or after-school treat.

Honey Lemon Squares

- » 1 stick butter
- » ¼ cup (60 ml) sucanat with honey—powdered
- » 1 cup (240 ml) plus 1 tablespoon whole wheat flour—soft pastry
- » ¾ cup (180 ml) honey
- » ½ cup (120 ml) lemon juice
- » 3 eggs
- » 1 teaspoon organic lemon peel—grated
- » ½ teaspoon baking powder

1. Preheat oven: 350°F (180°C).

2. Cream together butter and powdered sucanat until light. Add 1 cup (240 ml) of flour and mix well. Press mixture evenly into bottom of 9" square pan.

3. Bake for 15-20 minutes. Allow to cool for 20 minutes.

4. In medium bowl, whisk together 1 tablespoon flour with honey, juice, eggs, lemon peel, and baking powder until blended. Pour over the baked crust.

5. Bake 15-20 minutes more until filling is set. Cool in pan and cut into squares.

Orbappi Juice

» 2 cups (470 ml) nonfat yogurt
» 1 cup (240 ml) pineapple chunks
» 2 oranges—peeled, quartered
» 1 apple, cut into slices
» 1 banana; frozen works well also
» 1 tablespoon honey
» 2 cups (470 ml) ice

1. *Place ingredients in blender in the order given. Blend for 30-60 seconds on high.*

This recipe works best in a Vitamix blender. Enjoy with straws.

Freezing Bananas

Freezing bananas are a great way to avoid waste and to have frozen bananas for smoothies. Peel the banana first and then place in a zip lock freezer bag for storage.

Healthy Jell-O®

» 2 tablespoons unflavored gelatin
» A tiny pinch of stevia
» 1 tablespoon fruit juice
» 1 cup (240 ml) water—boiling
» 1 cup (240 ml) water—cold

1. *Dissolve gelatin, stevia, and fruit juice in hot water. Then add cold water. Refrigerate until set. Fresh fruit can be added.*

Harvest Coffee Cake

- » 2 cups (470 ml) cranberries
- » 1 cup (240 ml) chopped apple
- » 1 cup (240 ml) chopped nuts
- » ⅔ cup (150 ml) sucanat
- » ¼ cup (60 ml) applesauce
- » ¾ cup (180 ml) softened butter
- » ⅔ cup (150 ml) sucanat with honey or honey crystals
- » 3 eggs
- » 1 teaspoon vanilla
- » 1⅓ cup (315 ml) pastry flour
- » 1 teaspoon baking powder
- » ½ teaspoon salt

1. Preheat oven 350°F (180°C).

2. Sprinkle cranberries, apple, nuts, and ⅔ cup (150 ml) sucanat in a 9" x 13" pan.

3. Cream together applesauce, butter and ⅔ cup (150 ml) sucanat with mixer. Add eggs and vanilla; set aside.

4. Combine dry ingredients in a separate bowl then add to creamed mixture, mixing well. Drop batter by large spoonfuls over cranberry mixture.

5. Bake 35 minutes or until toothpick inserted in middle comes out clean.

Hummingbird Cake

- » 2 cups (470 ml) bananas—chopped
- » 1 cup (240 ml) apples—chopped
- » 3 cups (720 ml) whole wheat flour—soft pastry
- » 3 eggs
- » 1½ teaspoons vanilla
- » 1 teaspoon salt
- » 1 teaspoon baking soda
- » 8 ounces (224 g) crushed pineapple with juice
- » 1 cup (240 ml) nuts—chopped
- » 2 cups (470 ml) sucanat with honey
- » ⅓ cup (75 ml) olive oil
- » 1 cup (240 ml) dried unsweetened coconut
- » 1 teaspoon cinnamon
- » 1 cup (240 ml) butter

Preheat oven: 350°F (180°C).

1. *Mix dry ingredients in one bowl. Mix liquid ingredients in another. Combine the two.*

2. *Bake in a Bundt pan for 1 hour and 10 minutes.*

Delicious as is, but icing can be used for those who prefer extra sweet.

Impossible Pie

Simple and Satisfying

» ½ cup (120 ml) whole wheat flour—soft pastry
» ¼ teaspoon salt
» ½ teaspoon baking powder
» ½ cup (120 ml) honey
» ½ cup (120 ml) coconut—optional
» 4 eggs
» ½ stick butter—melted
» 2 cups (470 ml) buttermilk
» 1 teaspoon vanilla
» ¼ teaspoon cinnamon
» Dash nutmeg

1. Preheat oven: 350°F (180°C).

2. Mix in a blender and pour into an ungreased 10" pie dish. Sprinkle top with nutmeg.

3. Bake for 50-55 minutes. Good warm or cold.

Maple Syrup Strawberry-Rhubarb Pie

» 1 pie shell—unbaked
» 1 egg
» 1 cup (240 ml) whole wheat flour—pastry
» 1 cup (240 ml) maple syrup
» 2 cups (470 ml) rhubarb—chopped
» 1 cup (240 ml) strawberries—sliced
» ½ cup (120 ml) sucanat with honey
» ¼ cup (60 ml) butter
» ½ cup (120 ml) old-fashioned oats

1. *Preheat oven: 350°F (180°C).*

2. *Beat eggs and add flour, maple syrup, strawberries, and rhubarb. Pour into unbaked pie shell.*

3. *Mix together flour, oatmeal, sucanat, and butter. Spread over rhubarb and strawberries.*

4. *Bake for 45 minutes.*

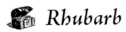 ## Rhubarb

Rhubarb is considered a vegetable, but it's most often treated as a fruit. Just like fresh cranberries, rhubarb is almost unbearably tart on its own and needs the sweetness of sugar, honey, or fruit juice added to it to balance out the acidity. Rhubarb's nickname is the "pie plant" because that is the primary use for this vegetable.

Peach-A-Berry Cobbler

- » 1 cup (240 ml) whole wheat flour
- » ½ cup (120 ml) sucanat with honey
- » 1½ teaspoons baking powder
- » ½ cup (120 ml) milk
- » ¼ cup (60 ml) butter—softened
- » ¼ cup (60 ml) sucanat natural
- » 1 tablespoon cornstarch
- » ½ cup (120 ml) cold water
- » 3 cups (720 ml) fresh peaches—sliced
- » 1 cup (240 ml) fresh blueberries
- » 1 tablespoon butter
- » 1 tablespoon lemon juice
- » 2 tablespoons sucanat with honey
- » ½ teaspoon nutmeg

1. *Preheat oven: 350°F (180°C).*

2. *Topping: Stir together flour, ½ cup (120 ml) sucanat with honey, and baking powder. Add milk and ¼ cup (60 ml) butter all at once. Stir until smooth. Set aside.*

3. *Filling: In a medium sauce pan stir together sucanat natural and cornstarch. Stir in water. Add peaches and blueberries. Cook and stir over medium heat until thickened and bubbly. Add 1 tablespoon butter and lemon juice. Stir until butter melts.*

4. *Pour into a 1½ quart (1.4 L) ungreased casserole. Spoon topping in mounds over hot filling. Spread evenly over filling. Sprinkle with mixture of 2 tablespoons sucanat and nutmeg. Place on a shallow baking pan in oven.*

5. *Bake cobbler for about 35 minutes or until bubbly and a toothpick inserted into crust comes out clean.*

   Serve warm with your favorite topping or ice cream.

Pumpkin Pie

- » 1 pie shell—unbaked—organic or make your own
- » 1-16 ounce (448 g) can or 2 cups (470 ml) pumpkin
- » 4 eggs
- » 1½ teaspoons cinnamon
- » ¾ teaspoon nutmeg
- » 1½ teaspoons vanilla
- » 1⅓ cups (315 ml) low fat milk
- » ½ cup (120 ml) honey
- » ¾ teaspoon ground ginger
- » ½ teaspoon salt

1. Preheat oven: 375°F (190°C).

2. Blend ingredients in blender. Pour filling into unbaked pie crust until reasonably full. Pour extra filling into a greased, oven-proof bowl.

3. Bake for about 45 minutes until set. Do not expect it to be fully firm in middle. It will firm up as it cools.

4. Keep refrigerated after cooling. Serve with fresh whipped cream.

Apple Butter

- » 7 cups (1.7 L) homemade applesauce
- » 2 cups (470 ml) apple cider
- » 1½ cups (360 ml) honey
- » 1 teaspoon cinnamon
- » ½ teaspoon ground cloves
- » ½ teaspoon allspice

1. Mix all ingredients in a crock pot. Cover and cook on low for 14 hours or until mixture is a deep brown.

2. Pack while hot into (4) four, hot pint (470 ml) jars.

3. Process in a hot water bath for 10 minutes, counting the time after the jars have been immersed and the water comes again to a rolling boil.

Pumpkin Spice Cake

A very tasty low fat cake that needs no frosting.

- » 1 cup (240 ml) sucanat
- » 4 tablespoons butter—softened
- » 1 cup (240 ml) pumpkin—canned, solid pack
- » 2 eggs
- » ½ cup (120 ml) yogurt
- » 1 tablespoon vanilla
- » 2 cups (470 ml) whole wheat flour—soft pastry
- » 2 teaspoons baking soda
- » 1½ teaspoons ground cinnamon
- » 1½ teaspoons ground ginger
- » ½ teaspoon allspice
- » 1 teaspoon baking powder
- » ½ teaspoon salt

1. Preheat oven: 350°F (180°C).

2. Spray a 13" x 9" glass baking dish with a non-stick spray, or use olive oil and liquid lecithin and spread around pan.

3. In large bowl, with mixer at high speed, beat sucanat and butter for about 2 minutes until well mixed, constantly scraping bowl with rubber spatula. Reduce speed to medium. Beat in pumpkin, eggs, yogurt, and vanilla extract. With mixer at low speed, add all dry ingredients. Beat just until well blended.

4. Pour batter into baking dish and spread evenly.

5. Bake cake for 25-30 minutes until toothpick comes out clean. Cool on wire rack.

Red Raspberry Streusel Pie

- » 1 cup (240 ml) yogurt—slightly strained
- » 1 egg
- » 1 teaspoon vanilla
- » ¾ cup (180 ml) sucanat with honey
- » 2 tablespoons whole wheat flour—soft pastry
- » ¼ teaspoon salt
- » 1 whole wheat 9-inch pie shell—unbaked
- » 1½ cups (360 ml) fresh or frozen raspberries
- » 3 tablespoons whole wheat flour—soft pastry
- » 2 tablespoons sucanat with honey
- » 3 tablespoons butter
- » 3 tablespoons pecans—chopped

1. *Preheat oven: 375°F (190°C).*

2. *Combine first 6 ingredients in a large mixing bowl. Beat at medium speed for 5 minutes or until smooth. Fold in raspberries. Spoon into a pie shell. Bake for 30 minutes or until set.*

3. *Combine 3 tablespoons flour and 2 tablespoons sucanat. Cut in butter with pastry blender until mixture resembles coarse meal. Stir in pecans.*

4. *Sprinkle mixture evenly over pie and bake 10 minutes until topping is lightly browned or slightly melted.*

Raspberries

Raspberries often appear as two crops; one in summer and another in autumn. Raspberries are fragile and must be handled gently. They can be eaten on their own or made into soups, purees, fine preserves, sorbets, and other desserts.

Sour Cream Pound Cake

- » 1 cup (240 ml) butter
- » 3 cups (720 ml) sucanat with honey
- » 1 cup (240 ml) sour cream
- » 3 cups (720 ml) whole wheat flour—soft pastry
- » ½ teaspoon baking soda
- » 1 teaspoon baking powder
- » 6 eggs
- » ½ teaspoon pure orange extract
- » ½ teaspoon pure vanilla extract

Frosting:
- » ¾ cup (180 ml) butter— softened
- » 3-4 cups (720-960 ml) powdered sucanat with honey
- » 1½ teaspoons almond extract

1. Preheat oven: 325°F (163°C).

2. Cream together butter and sucanat. Add sour cream. Sift flour, baking powder, and baking soda together in a separate bowl. Add dry ingredients to creamed mixture alternating with eggs. Add extracts.

3. Blend for 2 minutes. Pour cake batter in a greased and floured Bundt pan.

4. Bake for 1 hour and 20 minutes. Cool in pan for 10 minutes. Remove from pan and cool completely.

5. Frosting: Whip butter till light and fluffy, gradually adding sucanat and almond extract. Spread on cooled cake.

Sometimes special occasions call for a special treat. This cake is not low in calories but the ingredients are a better choice.

Pie Crusts

Graham Cracker Crust

- » 1½ cups (360 ml) whole wheat graham cracker crumbs
- » 2 tablespoons sucanat
- » ⅓ cup (75 ml) butter

1. Mix together and spread in pie pan.

Special Rice Pie Crust

- » 1½ cups (360 ml) brown rice flour
- » ½ teaspoon salt
- » ½ stick butter
- » ½ cup (120 ml) cold pineapple or orange juice for water

1. Preheat oven: 350°F (180°C).

2. Mix ingredients, place crust in pie pan.

3. Bake for 20 minutes.

Whole Wheat Single Pie Crust

- » 1¾ cups (420 ml) whole wheat flour—soft pastry
- » ½ teaspoon salt
- » ½ cup (120 ml) cold butter
- » 4 tablespoons ice water

1. Preheat oven: 425°F (220°C). (if pie requires a baked crust)

2. Blend with pastry blender: flour, salt, and butter until evenly mixed. Add water by tablespoons until crumbly. Gather dough together with hands, shaping into a ball but handling as little as possible. Pat out slightly on wax paper, place another piece wax paper over top and roll out. Place in a pie pan, trim and flute edges.

3. If crust is baked before filling, prick bottom and sides of crust with fork in several places. Bake for 8-12 minutes.

Whole Wheat Double Crust

- » 2¼ cups (530 ml) whole wheat flour—hard white or soft pastry
- » ¾ teaspoon salt
- » ⅔ cup (150 ml) butter—cold
- » 5 tablespoons ice water

1. *Prepare and bake as directed for single crust.*

Crunchy Oat-Nut Crust

- » ¾ cup (180 ml) flour
- » ½ cup (120 ml) quick oatmeal
- » ½ cup (120 ml) nuts—chopped
- » 2 tablespoons sugar
- » ¼ teaspoon salt
- » ½ cup (120 ml) butter—melted

1. *Preheat oven: 375°F (190°C).*

2. *Mix together thoroughly. Press into 9-inch plate. Bake for about 12 minutes. Cool before filling with any cold filling.*

Oatmeal Walnut Pie Crust

- » 1 cup (240 ml) old-fashioned oats
- » 4 tablespoons sucanat
- » ¼ teaspoon salt
- » ½ teaspoon vanilla
- » ⅓ cup (75 ml) butter—melted
- » ½ cup (120 ml) finely chopped walnuts

1. *Your choice allows you to bake this as the crunchy crust above or served cold like the recipe below.*

Oatmeal Coconut Pie Crust

» 1 cup (240 ml) oatmeal—quick cooking
» ½ cup (120 ml) sucanat
» ½ cup (120 ml) shredded coconut
» ⅓ cup (75 ml) butter—melted

1. Combine all ingredients in 9-inch pie plate. Mix well and press into sides and bottom evenly. Chill for ½ hour.

Oatmeal Pie Crusts With Apple

» 1 cup (240 ml) apple—grated
» ¼ cup (60 ml) oil
» ¼ cup (60 ml) nuts—chopped
» 2½ cups (530 ml) old-fashioned oats
» ½ teaspoon salt
» 1 tablespoon sucanat
» Water (if needed to make crumbly)

1. Preheat oven: 375°F (190°C).

2. Combine ingredients and mix well. Let stand to absorb moisture. Crumble half of mixture in the bottom of a greased pie pan. Press down firmly.

3. Bake for about 15 minutes or until brown and crisp. Fill with filling.

Makes 2 crusts.

Oatmeal Pie Crust

- » 1⅓ cups (315 ml) oatmeal
- » ⅓ (75 ml) cup sucanat
- » ⅓ cup (75 ml) butter—melted

1. *Preheat oven: 300°F (149°C).*

2. *Mix above ingredients together in mixing bowl. Then put in pie pan.*

3. *Bake for 15 to 20 minutes. Cover while baking.*

Two Oatmeal Pie Crusts

- » ½ cup (120 ml) butter—melted
- » ½ cup (120 ml) sucanat
- » 1 cup (240 ml) whole wheat flour—your choice
- » 1 cup (240 ml) quick oats

1. *Preheat oven: 300°F (149°C).*

2. *Mix together as for crumb crust and pat into pie pan.*

3. *Bake for 15 minutes. Cover while baking.*

Resources

Cookware—Royal Prestige—R.P. Spectrum, Inc.

888-80BRIDE, www.royalprestige.com—mention Designed Healthy Living for special pricing.

Vita Mix—Blender: Call 1-800-VITAMIX or 1-800-848-2649 or visit www.getvi-tamix.com Use this code for FREE shipping, a $25 value—06-003416

Food Co-op—www.quailcovefarms.com for East Coast deliveries, www.breadbeckers.com for east and south deliveries or for a co-op in your area go to www.localharvest.com.

Food Sources and Restaurants—www.localharvest.org, An information-packed website that gives you co-ops, markets, farms and other sources located in your area.

Cookbooks—*Wild Flour* by Denise Fidler is an excellent cookbook for learning to make your own breads. This cookbook can be found at www.countrybaker.com.

Bread Making Supplies and Grain Mills—Check out the Designed Healthy Living website for resources for all your bread making supplies.

Designed Healthy Living—www.designedhealthyliving.com

A website to give you lots of learning from the Healthy Living class. Plus a listing of future classes and on-line presentations. Check back often for updates and new recipes.

Consultations—Designed Healthy Living has a network of consultants who are trained in the Biblical design of our health, along with professional degrees in nutrition and health. Those who have purchased this book along with the Treasures of Healthy Living Bible Study are given a free 30-minute consultation for answers to food and supplement questions. To schedule an appointment call 1-804-798-6565 or e-mail: appointments@designedhealthyliving.com.

Discounts—4M Project It is the mission of Designed Healthy Living to make all resources available to those who are serving on the front line. 4M Project supports those in the top 4 areas making a difference in our world which includes military, ministries, missions, and ministers. If you are in any of these 4 service agencies, you can obtain resources from Designed Healthy Living, including supplements and organic cleaners, at a 35% discount. Please contact our office to get signed up for this on-going special. As long as you serve, we serve you.

Supplements and Protein—Shaklee is a health and wellness company that has been researching health and vitamins since 1915. There is no other company that can compare to the peer-reviewed research and studies Shaklee has accomplished. Their latest study conducted by the University of California, Berkeley, demonstrated how Shaklee vitamin users for 20 years had optimal health above those who took only a multivitamin or none at all. Read the peer-reviewed Landmark Study for yourself to investigate the value of Shaklee at www.landmarkstudy.com. To know more about this company go to www. reeder.myshaklee.com, or www.shaklee.com. If you have any questions or if you need help, please give our office a call 804-798-6565.

Organic Cleaning Products—www.shaklee.net/reeder/getclean

Guaranteed Proof—There are many companies to choose from in deciding to use these new, healthy products and ingredients, that it's easy to get confused. I was in the same situation many years ago. But I knew from working in the medical field for over 17 years that proof is necessary. This is why I strongly suggest you look for proof in the products you are buying. Second, look for a written unconditional guarantee. As I mentioned, the cookware I bought in 1980 has a lifetime warranty. The company has lived up to its reputation. Everyone should only buy from companies that have been in business a very long time and who can prove their products are the very best in the industry and contribute to long-term health. Don't be shy in asking for proof; your life depends on it.

Treasures of Healthy Living Bible Study
By Annette Reeder and Dr. Richard Couey

Everyone loves a treasure hunt. The hunt can be just as exciting as reaching the final treasure. This new adventure will follow the clues on our map and help us discover the answers to health to bring a life full of vitality. Watch as the counterfeits and substitutions that are currently robbing you of energy and zest are unveiled. Then what you find will fill the void with overflowing riches of health including delicious food, feelings of fulfillment, and a relationship real and personal. This Bible study will help you and your group use tools needed to reclaim health in the balance God designed. This book can be ordered through WinePressBooks.com or designedhealthyliving.com or by calling 1.877.421.7323.

Treasures of Health Nutrition Manual
Annette Reeder and Dr. Richard Couey

Are you tired of reading 50 books to find the answers to your health? This manual combines the nutrition from God-created foods with the value of vitamins to create a healthy and happy home and body. An encyclopedia of information is at your fingertips—a precious resource of information to treasure for years to come. This book can be ordered through WinePressBooks. com or designedhealthyliving.com or by calling 1.877.421.7323.

Bible Study Groups in Your Area

If you are interested in being part of a class in your area, please contact us for information. Classes are held in churches, at business locations, and in homes. A full series of inspirational and instructional DVD's and CD's are available at the Designed Healthy Living website. Watch the website for more information. (www.designedhealthyliving.com) I look forward to hearing from you and learning how God is blessing your health.

—Annette Reeder

Obtaining Optimal Health

The staff at Designed Healthy Living would like to thank you for purchasing this cookbook. It has been a delight to offer these recipes and cooking tips. Besides spending our days continuing our learning about health and cooking, we offer other services to our customers.

Have you tried changing foods, and cleaned up your home environment as much as possible, and are still dealing with health issues? Our team of certified nutrition consultants and advisors can assist you in determining the best route for obtaining optimal health. Everyone who has purchased the three books; *Treasures of Healthy Living Bible Study, Treasure of Health Nutrition Manual,* and this cookbook are eligible for a free consultation.

Call our office at 804-798-6565 to set up your appointment or e-mail at appointments@designedhealthyliving.com

Wishing you days of energy, years of great health, and a life of serving the Lord.

Index

INDEX

INDEX

INDEX

Other Books by Annette and Dr. Richard Couey:

Treasures of Health Nutrition Manual
Available soft cover and Kindle

Healthy Treasures Cookbook
Available soft cover

Daniel Fast
Available as download on website and Kindle

Many more to come - be watching and praying.

Designed Healthy Living

Changing lives one meal and a prayer at a time.

designed publishing

Designed Publishing Since 2004
Designed Healthy Living
Glen Allen, Virginia
804-798-6565
www.designedhealthyliving.com
Email: yourfriends@designedhealthyliving.com

formation can be obtained at www.ICGtesting.com
he USA
0260912

00003B/1/P